God, Are You Listening?

Tiffany Monroe

Copyrights

Table of Contents

God, Are You Listening?

Prologue

I was taught to pray early. In our home, prayer was woven into daily life before every meal, during every Bible study, our voices rising together in practiced reverence. But even then, I sensed that prayer could be something more. Somewhere in the quiet corners of my childhood, between the fears I carried in my small frame and the words I didn't know how to say aloud, I began to speak to God differently. Not just with words, but with sighs, questions, and that hollow ache in my chest I hoped only He could hear.

I didn't always know if He was listening. But I hoped He was. I needed Him to be.

Some nights, the prayers came like silent screams, muffled into my pillow. I asked Him to make my mother kinder. I begged for my father to stay home longer. I pleaded for the yelling to stop. For the morning to feel different. Better.

As I grew older, the prayers shifted. They became sharper, more direct less like ritual and more like reckoning.

Why did You put me here?

Why am I the one holding everything together?

Why does love hurt so much?

The answers didn't come the way I expected. There were no booming voices or clear signs. But in place of answers, I found moments. Quiet mercies. A classmate who always shared her crayons. An auntie who let me talk without rushing to fix me. Teachers who saw something good in me, even when I felt like I had nothing left to give.

And then there were the dreams—vivid, almost cinematic scenes that felt more like memories than imagination. I began to wonder if they were God's way of helping me remember truths I had forgotten. Truths buried beneath the silence. They reminded me I was more than what I had endured. That I still had a voice. A story worth telling.

This book is that story.

That whisper to God: Are You listening?

That whisper followed me through the years. And deep down, I think I always knew the answer.

Yes. He was.

Even when no one else saw me.

Even when I was too afraid to speak.

Even when the applause never came, and I had to find strength alone.

I was the girl who kept praying softly, steadily even when the answers were slow and the silence felt endless.

If you've ever wondered whether God hears the quiet ones the tired ones the ones holding everyone else together while falling apart inside... this is for you.

He heard me.

He hears you, too.

And maybe just maybe our stories can lead each other back to the light.

Chapter 1: Early Childhood

I came into the world on a cold February day in 1989, born at Kings County Hospital in Brooklyn, New York. My mother later told me I had to stay in the hospital for a while something about birth defects, though the details were vague and never fully explained. Even before I took my first breath at home, life seemed eager to test my strength. But I made it through small, quiet, but steadfast wrapped in God's mercy.

My name, much like my story, carries the fingerprints of those who came before me. It was my Aunt Yvette who chose Tiffany, inspired by the movie Breakfast at Tiffany's, a touch of elegance she hoped I'd carry with me. My mother added Aisha a name that once rested gently between the others, like a soft middle note in a melody. But somewhere along the way, Aisha disappeared. When I started kindergarten, my last name was changed, and Aisha vanished from the paperwork. Officially, I was left without a middle name. But in spirit, I never let it go. I still carry it unwritten but not forgotten.

There are only a handful of baby pictures, each one a silent clue to a story I've spent years trying to piece together. One shows me near a space aircraft exhibit just a small girl beneath the towering weight of the unknown. Another is from a McDonald's birthday party hosted by a white man I never recognized, his presence more puzzling than comforting. Then there's the photo of me with my father, taken just before my aunt's wedding. His arms are wrapped around me like a promise he didn't know how to keep.

Much of my early life feels like fragments faded images, scattered memories, incomplete stories. My mother rarely filled in the blanks, and when she did, her words came softly, in scattered bursts. Still, what I remember most wasn't the details but the atmosphere the sense of quiet resilience that surrounded us. Even in those blurry beginnings, I was being shaped. By love. By absence. By spirit.

It's as if God was already whispering over my life:

"This one will carry more than most. But she will carry it well."

Chapter 2: Houston Beginnings

Houston came into my life not as a decision, but as a destination I was carried to—somewhere between memory and mystery. I was around four or five when my mother returned to Brooklyn to bring me back with her. Until then, I had been staying with my grandparents, wrapped in the warmth of their care while the world shifted around me. My little brother had already been born in Houston, and I met him for the first time when I arrived. It felt like waking up in a story mid-sentence, trying to remember what came before.

I don't recall the flight or the moment we landed, but I remember the feeling. The buildings weren't towering and pressed together like Brooklyn's. The air was wider. The pace, slower. But everything felt unfamiliar. I couldn't name it then, but it was the beginning of a different kind of childhood—one where silence in the home often spoke louder than the voices in it.

We lived on the southwest side of Houston, tucked into a stretch of city where families led layered lives behind apartment walls. Inside our unit, everything was arranged just so. The sharp scent of cleaning products, the creak of plastic-covered couches, and glass figurines that caught the light like fragile hopes. Everything had its place. Everything looked right. But beneath the surface, something was always unsaid.

Years later, in that same city, I had a dream—or maybe something more. I was back in Brooklyn, in the room where it all began. I saw myself as a toddler, lying beside my grandfather. He started shaking violently. His eyes rolled back. I reached for him, tried to wake him, but he didn't respond. I screamed. My father and aunt came rushing in. Sirens followed. I was locked in a room while fire trucks and ambulances arrived. When the door finally opened, strangers praised me. Told me I had saved his life.

When I shared the dream with my mother, I described everything—the red brick building, the elevator with shiny brass buttons. She looked at me, puzzled. "How do you remember that?" she asked. "You were far too young." But I did remember. Not just the images—but the weight, the sound, the feeling. That dream stitched itself into my spirit like a memory God had hidden inside me, waiting to be revealed.

Shortly after that dream, my father received news that my grandfather had passed away. He flew back to New York for the funeral—but left me behind. I was furious. Something inside me broke. I had remembered him in my sleep, seen him leave this world. I wanted to say goodbye. I wanted to see if the photo he once showed me—in uniform, proud— was real. To know more about the man who once removed his wooden leg just to make me laugh. But I was left out, again.

Faith and confusion mingled in me like smoke in the wind. That dream had awakened something sacred. My earliest memory wasn't formed in waking life—but in sleep. A divine remembering. As if God had tapped me on the shoulder and said, You saw. You knew. You remember.

My parents both worked, though I couldn't tell you where. My father was present but distant, like a star you can see but never quite touch. I cherished every minute he gave me, even when it wasn't enough. My mother shifted more often. Some days she sang and smiled. Other days, I stayed quiet just to stay safe.

When my dad was home, reggae music filled the apartment—steady, soft. On weekends, we visited my aunt and uncle's houses, where the world seemed louder, warmer, realer. Laughter echoed through backyards, crawfish boiled on stoves, and music spilled out like joy that didn't need permission.

My brother—fragile and favored—quickly became the center of our world. His seizures were sudden and terrifying, unpredictable moments when his small body betrayed him and our home filled with panic. My mother would drop everything, rushing him to the emergency room with a fear louder than any siren. My father, calm but emotionally distant, didn't believe in doctors. He trusted nature and faith. Their arguments over what was best for my brother became a constant backdrop to our lives, a soundtrack of tension.

I remember the flashing ambulance lights. My mother's cries. The thick silence that settled in the walls long after the sirens faded.

One day, I pushed my brother too hard on the baby swing. It swung back and scraped the skin off my nose. I got in trouble—not for getting hurt, but for not being gentle enough with him. After that, I began hiding his things. Little acts of rebellion, quiet ways of expressing a confusion I didn't yet have words for. I wanted to matter again.

At the same time, my body was carrying its own silent distress. My eyes watered constantly. My nose ran for no clear reason. No doctor could explain it. My father handed me jars of raw honey and local pollen, urging me to take them daily. I did. Slowly, my symptoms faded. But my brother's trips to the hospital continued until he was almost nine—by then, the cracks in my parents' marriage had already taken root.

But school… school was different.

School made room for me.

I started kindergarten at Leistman Elementary in Alief. In the beginning, I couldn't read. My words were tangled—twisted by the Spanish I'd picked up from a babysitter in Brooklyn and the patchwork of Caribbean and New York accents that filled our home. Kids laughed at how I spoke, and eventually, I just stopped speaking altogether.

Speech therapy followed. Then books. Books became my refuge.

I read every *Cat in the Hat* I could find, and leaned into *Hooked on Phonics* like it held the key to being understood. And slowly, almost secretly, I found my voice again.

The gifted and talented program became my second home. I thrived there—in field trips, academic awards, extra projects that gave me permission to shine beyond the classroom. I remember the D.A.R.E. program, school plays where I danced in a poodle skirt, gymnastics routines under harsh gym lights. Boys teased me—poked me—because they liked me. At least, that's what we were told. And it made me feel noticed. Sometimes, even wanted.

One year, I scored perfectly on the TAAS test and earned the President's Award. I got to pie the principal in the face. The room burst into laughter, and for a moment, it felt like all the noise was for me. Another time, a painting I made for the Houston Rodeo won a prize. Those awards weren't just certificates or trophies. They were affirmations. Each one whispered, *I see you. You are good. You are enough.*

But the recognition I found in school didn't follow me home.

At home, I became small again.

We were Jehovah's Witnesses, which meant a strict schedule—meetings every Monday, Wednesday, Friday, and Sunday. Eventually, we added field service, study, and more meetings. At the Kingdom Hall, my mother smiled and chatted with the sisters. But at home, that smile vanished. Her words could cut. Her silence could settle like a storm cloud, waiting to break.

I had questions. Real ones.

Why does God let people suffer?

Why does love feel like pain?

But when I asked, I was hushed. Told to have more faith. So I began to wonder: if no one else saw me, maybe God did. Maybe He heard the parts of me that never made it into words.

I was afraid a lot. Of yelling. Of belts. Of the stories my parents told us about people who could take us away— people who wouldn't care for us. I lived with that fear in my chest like a second heartbeat.

But underneath it all was a quiet hope. A hope for peace. For gentleness. For someone to hold me without judgment.

So, I prayed.

Not the loud prayers said before dinner or during study, but the soft ones. The ones whispered through tears. The ones that slipped out in the silence of night, with no one listening but God.

Sometimes, it wasn't even words. Just longing. Just breath.

And in those moments, I believed He heard me. I *hoped* He saw me.

And slowly, I began to build the quiet belief that I was never truly alone. That even then—even in the confusion, the ache, the invisibility—God was holding me in ways I couldn't yet name.

Chapter 3: Light Between the Cracks

T hese years began to shape how I saw the world— and my place within it. I was still so young, but the ground beneath me was shifting. Home remained turbulent, but school became more than a place to learn. It became my shelter, a place where I could be seen without having to explain myself. I stayed on the honor roll and in the Gifted and Talented program, where I was encouraged to question, to imagine, to create.

In fourth grade, I found a rhythm of my own. I joined the school band's percussion section, and the sound of the drums grounded me. Every beat pulsing through my hands felt like a quiet reminder: *you're still here.*

My closest friend at the time wasn't a classmate—it was a teddy bear named Cuddles. He'd come from my aunt in Canada, a Christmas gift wrapped in softness and safety. Supposedly made of real fur, he became my confidant. I whispered to him when the house was too loud, held him close when I couldn't find the right prayers.

That Christmas was special—not just for the gifts, but because it was the first time I had my sister with me. She had just come from Grenada. Twelve years old and five years older than me, she looked so much like our mother it startled me. Her presence felt like a missing puzzle piece clicking into place—suddenly, I had someone who laughed with me, played with me, and made the house feel less like a battleground.

The night before Christmas, excitement got the best of us. We snuck into the living room and unwrapped one small gift each. I found a coloring book and crayons; she uncovered a Barbie. We carefully rewrapped them, hoping our little rebellion would go unnoticed. But the next morning, the joy was cut short. Our mother was furious. She said we had ruined Christmas—and refused to let us open anything else.

We spent the day in silence, tears soaking into the carpet. It wasn't until my father came home that something shifted. He spoke to her in a calm tone I rarely heard. Eventually, she allowed me to open one more gift. He brought me to the washing machine, lifted something from the top: a new bike, its handlebars gleaming under the dim light. That moment stayed with me—not just the gift, but what it symbolized. That joy could still show up in hard places.

That was also the only Christmas we ever had.

My mother was born in Grenada, one of the youngest in a family of twelve—eight sisters, four brothers. She was short, light-skinned, with long curly brown hair that framed her face like a crown. People said she looked like Tisha Campbell from *Martin*, especially when she dressed up— and she dressed up often. She had style: always in name brands, always polished. She put me and my sister in modeling gigs and etiquette classes, trained us to sit, smile, and speak like little ladies.

To others, she was radiant. Most of my friends thought she was Mexican—until they heard her speak. Her accent was a melody of Caribbean and New York, with bursts of Pig Latin that felt like some secret code. She was a year older than my father but carried herself like she had seen more, survived more, and done it with flair.

But her softness was selective. She poured it endlessly into my brother, showering him with affection and warmth. With me and my sister, she was sharp. Impatient. Often angry. I remember watching her cradle my brother, stroking his hair, laughing. Then turning to me with eyes that seemed to forget I needed love too.

There were moments of peace, but they never lasted.

Just before we moved to Sugar Land, one of those moments cracked. My mother discovered her treadmill was broken. She immediately blamed me and my sister. We denied it. She didn't believe us. For hours, we were yelled at, beaten, and forced to sit in our shame. We pleaded, but nothing softened her rage. When my father finally came home, he quietly asked my little brother what happened. He admitted it. He had broken it.

There was no punishment. Just silence.

I used to visit a little Asian girl who lived in the townhouse directly behind ours. After school, we'd walk to her place where her grandparents—an older Asian couple—always had rice and Spam cooking. The scent was strange but comforting. Yet behind the kitchen walls, their voices often turned sharp. Arguments escalated into something that felt dangerous, their words foreign and frantic. We'd sit on the floor and cover our ears.

Then, one morning, I woke to chaos. The complex was on fire. The flames spread to four homes, including ours. Our garage was damaged, but we got out safely—because I was the first to wake and alert everyone.

I never saw that family again. They vanished, like smoke.

Sugar Land was different. Quiet. Manicured lawns, matching houses, calm streets. But starting over wasn't easy. Because of how grades were arranged in the new district, I had to return to elementary school—despite having attended intermediate in Alief. I retook the TAAS test and passed again. The school offered to let me skip a grade. I felt proud. But my mother declined. She said she wanted to keep me around kids my age.

I nodded. But part of me wondered if I could've gone further. If I was being held back, in more ways than one.

Around that time, the fighting never stopped. The walls in our house were too thin to contain the fury. Her voice would rise—accusing, desperate, filled with pain I didn't yet understand. She'd follow him from room to room, screaming that he didn't love her, that he was cheating, that everything had been a lie.

Then something would break in him.

His silence would snap. He'd grab her, hands at her neck. Her voice would turn into gasps. His hands would strike her, over and over, until the sound of her crying went quiet.

And I—I would sit in the dark, breath caught in my throat, wondering if this time was the end.

My body always moved before I could think. I would run into the room screaming, jump on his back, throw whatever I could reach—anything to make him stop. Sometimes it worked. Sometimes he just walked out like nothing had happened. The door would slam, and the house would fall still, except for the sound of her crying and my heart pounding in my ears.

Afterward, I'd lie in bed, frozen and wide-eyed, wondering if God had heard me. Wondering if I had done enough. Wondering if it would happen again. And deep down, knowing it would.

My mother had an obsession with cleanliness that shaped the rhythm of our days. It wasn't just about tidiness—it was about control. Every surface had to shine. Every corner scrubbed until it reflected her face. If it wasn't perfect, we started over. Sometimes we cleaned the same room for hours, repeating motions until her mood shifted or she ran out of energy.

My sister and I became her hands, her runners. She'd call us from across the house just to pass her the remote—even if it sat inches from her fingers. I handled the laundry, folding and sorting piles that never seemed to shrink. My sister took charge of the kitchen, helping prepare meals our mother seasoned and froze in exact portions—labeled, dated, lined up like soldiers in the freezer.

My brother never lifted a finger. He was excused, protected—the prince of our house.

I don't think she meant to break us down with the discipline. But there wasn't much room left for tenderness. Her love was a quiet reward you earned through obedience. A clean room. A finished task. Silence.

So, I searched for ways to stay away.

I signed up for lessons at the neighborhood club— swimming, tennis, basketball—anything that would keep me out of the house. I joined every activity I could. I just needed more space to breathe.

That's when I met Courtney.

My classmates used to say we looked like sisters and often called me by her name. She lived about a mile away, in a two-story home that always smelled like sweet tea and old records. She had two older brothers, a mother and father who were always present, and an elderly Black housekeeper who adored Michael Jackson and kept glass bottles of Coca-Cola in the fridge just for us.

Her dad played in a jazz band. Her mother was a doctor— tall, elegant, always in professional clothes with a sharp bob, red lipstick, and matching nails. I was mesmerized. She felt like the kind of mother I had prayed for.

When things got bad at home, I'd run to their house. Sometimes her mom would call mine and calmly say I'd be staying with them until things cooled down. And somehow, that always worked.

Their house felt like a different world. Safe. Creative. Full of air.

Courtney's family stayed with me. Her mom became a second mother, someone I could look up to when I felt small. I used to wish she would adopt me. Maybe then I could finally breathe.

Those years taught me to hold onto joy wherever I found it, to search for the quiet places where light slipped through the cracks, and to keep listening for something sacred beneath all the noise.

Chapter 4: The Echo of My Own Voice

At home, things were slowly unraveling. My dad had started working overseas—St. Thomas, Kosovo, Afghanistan, Ethiopia, Dubai. We only saw him a few times a year, usually when he returned to sweep us away on luxurious vacations that made everything feel okay, if only for a little while. We visited London to meet one of his cousins, then Jamaica and Grenada, where the air hung thick with history and heritage. We took cruises. We saw Niagara Falls in Canada and visited his siblings in Toronto and Montreal. Every summer, we returned to New York to be with my grandmother and the rest of his family. There were congregation meetings, too—tours of massive Jehovah's Witness factories that somehow felt both awe-inspiring and suffocating. In those moments, it felt like we could breathe again. Like life had briefly loosened its grip.

My father had a presence that turned heads. Tall, dark-skinned, with thick glasses and a grin wide enough to hold a room, he moved through the world like someone who belonged in the spotlight. People mistook him for Wesley Snipes in airports and grocery stores. Strangers would ask for autographs, and he'd sign them with a quiet wink. When I asked why, he said, "They think I'm famous… maybe I am." Overseas, he brushed shoulders with politicians and celebrities. Sometimes, he'd call during performances on military bases and hand the phone to someone—Coolio once said hello. Another time, he Skyped me while standing beside President George Bush. He sent back gifts from every corner of the world: porcelain dolls, gold jewelry, black diamonds, even a doll stitched with golden thread from a King in Africa. He listened to reggae and drank his beers with a laugh that made everything feel lighter. And yet, he was also the man who dropped me off at school in his ancient red car that rumbled like a broken drum. Still, there was magic in how he talked about the future: "One day we'll go to the motherland, grow dreads, and feel the sun on our skin the way it was always meant to." With him, the world felt bigger, like anything was possible.

But when he left, it was just us—and my mother. She had become a stay-at-home mom, and the quiet anger inside her had started leaking out like smoke under a door. Her mood swings turned sharp, stormy, and my sister and I were caught in the blast. I tried to protect my sister, but it always cost me something. My mother told everyone I was the problem child, disrespectful. But I wasn't trying to cause trouble. I was trying to survive.

Middle school came like a shift in the wind. We were still in Sugar Land. I still rode my bike with pegs, still skated the streets just to feel something close to freedom. But something inside had begun to change. My days became a blur—volleyball and track practice in the early morning, school, then cleaning, homework, dinner, and often Bible study. The structure kept me moving, but in the quiet spaces between the noise, the silence started to hum louder.

I started at Garcia Middle School, where I was placed in band. My percussion background from elementary school caught my teacher's eye. He pushed me, challenged me, and I rose to it. Rhythm was still my refuge—a pattern I could control, a beat that made sense when nothing else did. At lunch, hip hop was on the rise. We tapped pencil beats on the cafeteria tables, our own little stage, and it felt like a kind of rebellion. A kind of belonging.

That summer, I joined the swim team to face a fear I had buried deep. The last time I swam was back in Alief, when my dad decided to teach me the only way he knew how. "Fish don't need no lessons," he said. Then he tossed me into the deep end. I panicked, kicked, gasped, prayed—and somehow made it out. After that, I avoided water completely.

But something inside me whispered: *try again.* On the first day of swim team, the coach told us to jump in and freestyle. I could barely doggy paddle, but he didn't send me away.

Instead, he took time to teach me. Within weeks, I was gliding through the water, winning races, collecting medals. It felt like healing.

Then came the butterfly race. I swam with everything I had—and won. But instead of cheers, I heard hate. A man screaming at his daughter: *"How could you let a nigger beat you?"* My mother lost it. She yanked me away, shouting, protective and furious. I never swam competitively again. It wasn't just the word that broke me. It was the moment I realized that no matter how hard I tried, the world could still spit me out.

That fall, a new school opened nearby, and I transferred. With my best friend by my side, I threw myself into everything—volleyball, basketball, track. I even volunteered with the gifted and talented program to help students with disabilities. That year, I started to feel it: the pull toward the person I was meant to become. Capable. Strong. Seen.

I had my first boyfriend that year. His name was Jacob. He was Jewish and brave enough to ask my mother if we could date. She said no, of course. I wasn't allowed to have friends outside of school. But we found our way—sneaking out after school for slices of pizza, talking like the world was ours. It felt innocent and enormous at the same time. We broke up after I refused to kiss him in front of our friends. I wasn't ready. Not for that.

Through it all, I prayed. I studied the Bible more deeply. I prepared for baptism. I wasn't just going through the motions—I was trying to prove I was worthy of something sacred. I still had my dreams, vivid and strange, like messages from somewhere beyond. My mom played Kingdom melodies in the house and car. Sometimes, they brought comfort. Other times, they felt like background music for a life I wasn't sure was mine.

Even when I questioned what was real, even when it felt like no one saw what I was carrying—I still believed in God. I needed to. My faith didn't fix everything, but it helped me hold on. Not because it was perfect, but because it was mine. It gave me something solid to grip when the world felt like water, trying to drown me.

These were the years I began to hear my own voice—not loud, not fully formed, but there. A voice asking to be seen. A voice that prayed, even when no one else knew. A voice that danced on cafeteria tables and whispered through dreams. A voice that belonged to me.

Chapter 5: Between the Notes

My sister ran away from home. She was a junior in high school was full of rebellion, fire, and exhaustion. I had watched my sister for years as she pushed against the suffocating walls of our house—sneaking phone calls with boys, staying late after school, scribbling in journals she guarded like treasure maps. The yelling, the beatings, the endless demands—eventually, it all wore her down. One night, without warning, she packed a small bag, climbed out through my bedroom window, and disappeared into the night. I watched her go, frozen in silence.

I wasn't just scared for her—I was scared for me. Her escape meant I inherited everything she left behind: her chores, her blame, her place beneath our mother's fury. My brother, sensing the new dynamic, slipped into entitlement, parroting the same disrespect that had once been hers. The house didn't grow quieter after she left. The storm just changed direction.

Middle school became a kind of melody—quiet, steady, a rhythm that carried me. I moved between the sharp lines of sheet music and the blur of basketball courts. I was still in band, now advanced enough to play alongside high school musicians. My hands were trained and precise, and there was something sacred in sound—something older than words, something that felt like it belonged to me.

Outside of music, I pushed my body in every way I could: volleyball, basketball, track. I even tried out for the football team, one of only two girls who dared to believe we belonged. My mom shut that down quickly. "Football isn't for girls like you," she said. Still, I kept moving. I kept showing up.

Courtney was my tether. Our friendship was stitched together with jump shots, mixtapes, and shared hunger—for peace, for escape, for meaning. Her house became my soft landing when mine turned hard and sharp. Her brothers took us in like little sisters. They taught us basketball and music, rhythm and resilience. Zeke played guitar and helped me record my first songs. I was learning how to stretch my voice beyond the limits of our walls. Limewire. MySpace. Headphones and late nights. I wasn't just surviving—I was creating something. A doorway. A signal.

One day, we sent a track to a music producer. He wanted to sign me. Just like that, a dream cracked open. But my mother said no. And just like that, it shut again.

At school, I wore Baby Phat and Rocawear—rhinestone jeans, velour tracksuits in every color, fresh white Air Force 1s with oversized laces, lip gloss thick enough to leave a glitter trail. My hair was permed, braided, cornrowed with beads that clicked when I walked, or twisted into a curly mohawk. Our backpacks were too big for our bodies and stuffed with flip phones, roll-on glitter, and secrets. Fashion was more than style—it was armor. It was the way we spoke when speaking felt dangerous. My reflection became my statement, and sometimes, my shield.

As a Jehovah's Witness, I didn't celebrate birthdays or holidays. I wasn't invited to many parties, and when I was, I had to say no. I didn't want to be left out—I just didn't know how to explain the shape of my world.

Home was quieter now, but not peaceful. My mother still favored my brother. I was expected to tutor him, clean up after him, and take the hits—verbal and otherwise—when his temper snapped. His words cut deeper than his fists, and I learned the art of avoidance. I wanted calm. But I had to make it for myself.

So I built it—out of music, writing, and midnight creativity. I taught myself how to build websites, layered my own beats, recorded over old cassette tapes. I snuck onto the computer at 2 a.m., mixing hope and heartbreak into sound. I dreamed of performing. Of being seen. Of not having to explain.

And still, even then, I prayed.

God wasn't just a name. He was a hiding place, a whisper I clung to when no one else could hear me.

Some mornings, I knocked on classmates' doors with Bible tracts in hand, pretending it wasn't strange to be standing on their porches. Field service was required. I smiled awkwardly as my peers stared through me with polite confusion.

In class, we started learning about the Holocaust. Something about that history gripped me—especially the stories of Jehovah's Witnesses who refused to recant their faith, even in camps. I poured myself into a research project. My parents took me to Washington, D.C., to the Holocaust Museum. I interviewed a survivor. Built a display board as tall as my dreams. Something awakened in me—a desire to understand where I came from. Who I really was, beneath the beliefs that were handed to me.

I started digging into the silences of our family history. At each aunt's house, I'd sift through old photo albums like sacred texts. Faded images of a grandfather and grandmother I never met surfaced like ghosts. They said she fell from a tree and died on the island. Six months later, her husband died too—some said from heartbreak. They had twelve children, raised in a plantation-style house in Grenada. The home was small. The stories, heavy.

Sometimes the adults spoke in pig Latin to keep secrets, but I learned to understand. I was studying their language. Their wounds.

In New York, I found more fragments. My grandmother had a photo of my grandfather in his Royal Grenada Police Force uniform. My dad appeared in an old soccer uniform—his legs scarred with pride. They told me how the U.S. invaded Grenada in 1983 after the Prime Minister's assassination. That's when the family scattered. Some fled to Brooklyn. Others to Virginia and Texas. My grandfather had more children than anyone could count. My dad was the youngest of nine.

Even love touched me, briefly. Folded notes passed in hallways. Soft glances across classrooms. Nothing serious—

my mother's rules forbade it. But the longing sat quietly inside me, tucked in lyrics and scribbled lines.

And still, I believed. In God. In music. In the invisible thread that pulled me toward a future I couldn't name yet. Somewhere between the drumline and the prayer line, I was becoming someone. Someone who would one day break the silence for good.

Chapter 6: Kingdoms and Crutches

We moved again. A bigger house, still in the same neighborhood, but now even farther from Courtney. Too far to bike. Too far to run to when things got loud. My sister was still gone. My brother was growing up and growing meaner. And my mom seemed to redirect all her old anger toward me.

High school hit like a wave I didn't know how to swim in. Stephen High School was bigger, louder—a maze of unfamiliar hallways and rules I didn't yet understand. I stepped in as a freshman still clutching the rhythms of middle school in one hand, while the other reached toward the demands of this new, faster world.

I kept my spot in band, volleyball, and basketball for a while—clinging to music as my refuge and sports as my escape. But eventually, they made me choose. I chose movement. I chose the court. I think part of me wanted to run—not just across the gym floor, but away from the limits of my home, my body, my life.

At school, I had teammates and classmates—laughter during practice, whispered conversations in locker rooms, group projects with kids who seemed older and sharper. But that's where the connection ended. No birthday parties. No sleepovers. My mom only allowed overnights at Courtney's, and even those were rare.

Trevor was the closest thing I had to a high school romance. He sat next to me in public speaking, his voice warm and buttery like a 90s R&B track. He'd sing to me between classes, our hands brushing in crowded hallways. Sometimes, he'd ride my bus home just to walk me to my door, then turn around and trek miles back to his. Once, my mom caught us on one of those walks. I thought it was over. But after pleading with both sets of parents, we were allowed to stay friends—with strict supervision. So there we were: watching Disney movies on the couch while my mom sat inches away. It wasn't much, but it was something. Until he moved to Beaumont. We tried the long-distance thing, but it unraveled quickly.

Courtney and I were still sisters in spirit, but the air between us was changing. She leaned into the varsity crowd—popular, fearless, free. I leaned into advanced courses and teammates who lived in that safe middle ground. We were still parallel, but the space between our paths widened.

Home was getting worse. I told my dad something was wrong. My youngest uncle came to stay with us. At first, I didn't understand. He was different—distant, almost mechanical. He could sit still for hours, chanting in strange languages. One night, I woke to find him standing in my doorway, pointing and screaming for the devil to leave my room. I froze. The fear soaked into me like cold water. After that night, he was gone.

Later, I learned he had schizophrenia. The family split—some wanted him institutionalized, others, like my mom, refused to believe he was sick. I started researching, learning the symptoms, reading the stories, trying to explain to her that it could be genetic. She brushed me off, but soon I noticed her taking what I called her "happy pills." When they kicked in, she'd go on shopping sprees, smiling more. But the warmth never lasted.

Then came the injury. During basketball practice, I was pushed while shooting a three-pointer and landed wrong, tearing my MCL. The pain was sharp, but the fear was sharper. I was already on JV—would this take it all away? My mom picked me up from school and drove me to the hospital. Then came weeks on crutches. No running. No playing. No escape.

That's when I met Aaron—caramel skin, brown eyes that melted me. The crutches slowed my pace between classes, and he, as a sports assistant, often stayed behind after games.

We kept running into each other in the hallways. He'd carry my bag, slip me folded love poems, handwritten songs. His ROTC uniform, with its neat rows of badges, seemed to fit the way he carried himself. One day, he handed me a note with boxes to check: "Will you be my girlfriend?" I drew a heart and wrote "maybe." I guess he took it as no, because soon after, he started dating one of my friends.

Healing came, slowly. That summer, thanks to Courtney's parents, I joined an AAU basketball team. I trained hard, rebuilt strength, and found a new rhythm in my body. I started to believe I might make it out.

My faith still threaded through my life. I attended meetings, went out in field service. My mom encouraged me to join teen Witness outings—as if I were being put on display for marriage. It left me feeling appraised rather than appreciated.

Inside, though, questions were growing. My dreams were filled with Queens—warriors draped in gold, cloaked in wisdom. I read about royal women locked in towers who still wielded power. I began to see myself as one of them—not a fairy tale princess, but a spiritual one. Royal blood, trapped in a dungeon, waiting.

That realization didn't set me free, but it anchored me. It reminded me I was more than the roles I played. More than the hurt I carried. More than the silence I swallowed.

And my story was still being written.

Chapter 7: Cracks in the Crown

By junior year, I was clawing toward freedom like a wounded animal gasping for air—still bleeding hope from a thousand small cuts.

Trevor drifted back into my life for a brief, flickering moment. We dated again, but time had changed us. He ended it in the middle of the hallway, in front of everyone. It was cruel, deliberate, public. Whispers swirled through the air—rumors that I had cheated, that I was too much. But when the noise faded, we talked. I cried. He listened. We parted without hate. That quiet mercy stayed with me.

Then Hurricane Katrina hit, and the world shifted. The halls filled with voices from New Orleans—fast, electric, alive. It changed the air. I made friends among them, but my connections stayed shallow. Courtney and I drifted further apart. She rose as a varsity starter, a queen surrounded by older girls and louder parties. There were whispers about her too—things I didn't understand then. Our bond thinned, but her parents remained steady. They came to my games when my own mother never did, their cheers filling the empty space in my bleachers. The only constant was Aaron, camera in hand, filming every play.

Home was no refuge. It was a minefield. I moved like a shadow, dodging my mother's moods and my brother's cruelty. I begged my father to see me, to believe me—but he always chose her side. I carried the weight of being cast as the villain in a story I never wrote.

Still, there were promises I clung to like fragile glass. My father once said, "Straight A's, and I'll buy you a car." That single sentence became my life raft. I poured everything I had left into earning those grades. And I did it.

But the day it arrived, it wasn't what I imagined.

I stepped off the school bus and froze. There in the driveway was a black Volkswagen Beetle, polished to perfection, topped with a giant red bow. My stomach sank. Everyone else smiled; I burned. I had dreamed of something sleek, bold—me. This felt like a costume I didn't want to wear. "I'll never drive that," I said flatly.

It sat untouched for days until it vanished. Then my mom took me to a Nissan dealership and traded it for a brand-new blue Altima. I had begged for a Mustang, something with bite. She said the insurance was too high. Weeks later, Courtney got one—a black Ford Mustang. "Close enough," my mom shrugged. It wasn't mine, but it didn't matter. We had wheels. We had freedom.

We tore through half-built roads in Sugar Land like they were ours—no rules, no limits. Asphalt stretched wide and wild, carrying our laughter into the night. It was the closest thing to flying we had ever known.

Then came Stefon. I met him at a Witness camping trip in Lake Charles—a Black cowboy with warm eyes and a quiet voice. He promised me a horse. We studied the Bible together. He asked for my hand in marriage, gave me a ring. My parents said no. Another dream dangled, then cut loose.

I begged my father to move me—to an international school, to my grandmother's house, anywhere else. I even toured a school in New York, freedom tucked into every stairwell and hallway. But no one said yes. I stayed in Texas—a caged bird learning to sing in silence.

I returned to basketball, rebuilt myself after my torn MCL, and made varsity. That summer, AAU brought me to the Houston Elites. I hadn't planned it. I came to watch Courtney, but as I sat in the bleachers, every bounce of the ball thudded against my chest. Every swish called to something I couldn't quiet.

When the court cleared, I laced up and started shooting. Jumpers, one after another—clean, crisp, controlled. Everything Courtney's brother had drilled into me poured out like water breaking through a dam.

The coach noticed. He didn't wave me off—just watched. Then he asked my name. I told him the truth: I wasn't on any list, hadn't been invited, but I wanted a shot. His nod cracked open a door I thought was sealed shut. That day, I became a Houston Elite.

They didn't put me on the all-star team—Courtney had that spot. Instead, I landed on the second team, and it turned out to be a gift. No shadows. No comparisons. Just me, seen and shining.

That season changed me. I was a starter. A scorer. A competitor. Basketball stopped being just a game—it became a reclamation. Every drop of sweat, every bruise, every win felt like worship.

One coach—tall, dark, built like a retired pro—believed in me before I believed in myself. He drove me to tournaments when my parents wouldn't. He cheered from the sidelines when no one else came. His name may blur in memory someday, but not his impact. He was a quiet answer to my oldest prayer: *See me. Choose me. Fight for me.*

And then there was Cynthia. Short, dark-skinned, built for speed—she ran point while I played shooting guard. Together we were a storm. Her passes always found me; mine always found her. It was magic, pure and unspoken. But what I remember most wasn't just the game—it was her mother. She came to every match, her cheers the loudest in the gym. When she saw me eating lunch alone, she began bringing me food—home-cooked meals wrapped in foil and care. It wasn't just nourishment. It was belonging.

Eventually, they welcomed me like family. I started spending afternoons at Cynthia's place, slipping into her world as easily as putting on a favorite sweatshirt. We went to teen parties together, met her cousins—rappers, DJs, even a few names I'd heard on the radio. It was swagger and sound, a rhythm I didn't know I'd been missing. For the first time in years, I felt like I belonged somewhere that wasn't a basketball court.

At her house, I watched Cynthia and her mom laugh like sisters. The way they teased each other, the way her mom's affection was effortless—it stirred something in me I couldn't name at the time. I didn't just want their life; I wanted their ease. That softness. That steady, unconditional love.

And then—like so many times before—the good cracked.

Scholarship offers came. Real offers. Doors I'd been fighting to open since middle school. But every single one was out of state. My mother said no. Just like that, the golden doors slammed, their light snuffed out before I could step through.

Spiritually, I was unraveling. Not because I was running from God, but because I was starving for Him. Basketball became my altar. Sweat became prayer. But my mother didn't see devotion; she saw idolatry. She said I had made the court my god.

And then came the night the walls caved in.

My father came to visit—a rare, uneasy event. The air felt tense before he even stepped inside. They started arguing almost immediately, words ricocheting like bullets through the house. I stood between them more than once, arms out, begging them to stop. He paced, fists clenched. She matched him word for word, her voice flaring higher with every breath.

Then—my name. Shouted from downstairs. Sharp. Broken.

I ran.

He stood in the doorway, frozen, eyes wide, a kitchen knife buried near his wrist. Blood darkened his sleeve. Then he crumpled.

I dropped beside him, screaming. My hands were shaking so badly I almost dropped the phone when I tried to call for help. My mother appeared from the bedroom—charging, not checking. My little brother ripped the phone from my hands and yelled into the receiver, "My mom stabbed my dad!"

The rest was a blur—sirens, red-blue lights flickering against our quiet Sugar Land Street, EMTs leaning over my father, neighbors peering through blinds. My dad refused to leave, told the police not to press charges. But it didn't matter—they cuffed her anyway.

When they led her out, her eyes locked on mine. Cold. Accusing. As if I had put the knife in her hand.

She was released the next day, but the truth was carved into me now. I wasn't safe. None of us were. And no amount of church meetings could explain how someone could claim righteousness while bleeding out their spouse in the kitchen.

Senior year came draped in loss. First Aunt Yvette—my gentle light, my quiet refuge. Her attic was a studio where walls bloomed with color and her husband painted me into storybooks. She made me feel chosen. At her funeral, I stood shaking at the podium, asking God why He'd take the one safe place I had left.

Not long after, my uncle was gone too—hit by drag racers on his way to refill his medication. My mother had to identify him. She came back silent.

Grief sat on my chest. I started slipping.

One day, I drank Everclear at school, thinking I could handle it. I couldn't. I lost time, lost my footing—woke in the nurse's office feeling like a ghost. My mother kicked me out for refusing to skip my last basketball game for a Kingdom Hall meeting. She tossed my gym bag on the porch like garbage. My sister picked me up without asking questions.

At school, my counselor called me in. I braced for scolding, but instead, she told me my future was mine to claim—that my past didn't have to decide it. Something in me shifted. I pulled my grades up, graduated in the top 10% of my class.

Living with my cousin was oxygen. I worked on music, built an online following, and landed an A&R gig at a local studio. It wasn't glamorous—faded signage, cracked tile floors—but inside? Magic. The walls vibrated with basslines and verses, the air thick with weed smoke and wood polish.

I learned fast—scouting talent, organizing sessions, giving feedback. They called me "Stargirl." For the first time in a long time, my voice mattered. That studio wasn't just work; it was sacred space. A place where raw sound could heal.

I started modeling again. This time, for me. But one booking turned into something darker. I met with a photographer at his apartment—a makeshift studio with cheap backdrops and props. He poured me wine. That's the last thing I remembered. I woke up clothed, $100 by my side, trust ripped from me.

Prom came. I had no dress, no date. My aunt urged me to go. I asked Adrian, a friend from AAU, last-minute. We danced, laughed, and that night, I lost my virginity. We dreamed of parallel careers—him in the NBA, me in the WNBA—before distance pulled us apart.

My mother let me move back in for show, just long enough for family to see me "safe" at graduation. The moment the aunt left, the cruelty returned. I left again—back to my cousin's, back to something like home.

I had survived.

Not just school. Not just heartbreak.

But rejection, spiritual exile, loss, and the deaths of too many dreams.

And still

I was here.

I was rising.

I was scared.

Chapter 8: Shadows After the Stage

Graduation didn't feel like freedom. It felt like standing at the edge of a cliff—no wings, no parachute, no one waiting to catch me. Just me, holding a diploma in one hand and an unshakable question in the other: *What now?*

After the cheers faded and the principal's handshake was already a blur, I was back at my sister's house, staring at that paper like it was a ticket to somewhere I couldn't afford to go.

With school behind me, my sister and cousin made it clear: time to work. No more late mornings. No more living in daydreams. I tried to follow the script—filled out college applications, my sister covering the fees—and to my surprise, the acceptance letters rolled in. But the illusion shattered when I realized I couldn't even enroll without my parents' financial information. On paper, I was still a dependent. In reality, I was already on my own. And I knew they wouldn't help. They never had.

So, I turned back to the only thing that had ever made me feel fully alive—music.

That's when he appeared. The rapper. Older, magnetic, his presence pulling people into his orbit. He was the brother of someone I knew at the recording studio where I worked as an A&R. When he spoke, his words curled in the air like smoke; when he performed, he carried the crowd in his palm. Standing next to him, I felt like I belonged in a world that had always been just out of reach.

With him came a new kind of freedom—underage club entries, VIP booths, nights lit by strobe lights and the thump of bass under my skin. I modeled in music videos. I remixed Boosie's *Wipe Me Down* and, for the first time, heard my own voice echo back from a crowd.

My mother's angry voicemails became background noise—sermons about shame, warnings about "the Devil's playground." But I wasn't running from God. I was searching for Him in places I'd never looked before. So, when my boyfriend handed me a Quran and told me to open my mind, I did. Not as a rejection of my faith, but as an act of curiosity.

And then—he disappeared.

One missed call, one night where he didn't show, and suddenly the connection unraveled. Instead of moping, I went out with my sister and her friends to a Caribbean party. We laughed, danced, let strangers buy us drinks.

The next morning, I woke up to blood.

It was bright, unnatural—wrong. My sister brushed it off as too much alcohol, but something deep in me whispered no. I begged her to take me to the ER. She told me to lie, to say I was pregnant so they'd see me faster.

The lie uncovered the truth.

When the nurse turned the monitor toward me, her expression changed. Her eyes startled.

"I'm not pregnant," I said quickly. "I can't be."

She didn't argue. She just left the room.

When she came back, she asked a blur of questions before finally saying:

"You were pregnant—with twins. You lost one."

The words hit like lightning. My breath stopped. My limbs trembled. I ripped the IV from my arm. I wanted to run, but there was nowhere to go.

When I woke again, another nurse sat beside me, holding a calendar. A monitor beeped in the corner. "That's your baby's heartbeat," she whispered.

Everything inside me went still.

I was 23 weeks along—almost six months. And it was a boy.

My mind raced. *Who?*

I called Adrian, my prom date. He was kind but certain—*not me.* Then I called the rapper. He laughed, said he already "felt something was off," like it was a joke.

We traced the dates on the calendar. They landed on April. The photo shoot. The makeshift backdrop. The wine glass of "water." Waking up on a stranger's couch, sore and confused. The moment I had buried now screamed through every cell in my body.

I called him—the photographer. Too weak to speak, I handed the phone to the nurse. She asked if we were dating. He stammered, laughed nervously, said "kind of." It was enough.

"You're the father," she told him.

He picked me up from the hospital. I sat in his car like a ghost. I didn't yet have the language for what had been taken. I didn't know the term *date rape*. I only knew my silence carried a weight I couldn't set down.

When my mother found out I was pregnant, she pulled me back in—not with love, but with control. She arranged doctor visits with the man I now hated. She told me abortion was against our faith. She urged me to marry him.

But where was faith when I cried myself to sleep? Where was God when my body was no longer my own?

My mother even threw me a baby shower. Invited his family from New Orleans. Smiled like this was something sacred, like this pregnancy was a blessing to be celebrated.

The whole thing felt like a ceremony I hadn't agreed to. She planned every detail—decorations, food, invitations—as if this were *her* moment of redemption. To her, it was a celebration. To me, it was a performance. A way to dress up a truth we weren't speaking. To make me look like the dutiful daughter, the glowing mother-to-be, while inside I was coming apart.

The house swelled with people—relatives I hadn't seen in years, unfamiliar faces from his side of the family. They arrived carrying wrapped boxes and polite smiles, placing them on the gift table like offerings. The room buzzed with laughter and conversation, but I felt separate from it all, like I was watching someone else's life. My hands rested on my stomach—round now, undeniable—while every coo and "congratulations" slid over me like a lie.

The baby's father sat beside me, performing his role. Smiling for photos. Resting his arm around me. Offering thanks. But between us was a silence so deep it hummed. There was no bond, no love, no shared joy—only a secret neither of us wanted to hold. And I didn't dare break the illusion. My mother had invested so much in it, and I didn't have the strength to undo her work.

At one point, she stood to pray over the baby. Her voice shifted into the tone she used for the congregation—formal, measured—thanking Jehovah for this "new blessing" and "fresh start." I stared at the floor, asking God in silence if He was even listening. Was this His plan? Or was I carrying the weight of someone else's mistake, dressed up as destiny?

The gifts piled high—diapers, blankets, onesies, baby books. Applause followed each unwrapped item, but inside I was unraveling. I kept thinking: *I don't even know if I want to be a mother. I didn't choose this. I didn't ask for this life.* And no one had asked me anything.

Somewhere in the noise and celebration, something else was happening—something I wouldn't understand until much later. My cousin, the one who'd taken me in after my mother kicked me out, was laughing in the corner with one of my baby's father's cousins. They exchanged numbers. Smiles lingered. Without knowing it, they were planting the seeds of a relationship that would grow into something beautiful for them. It's strange how life works—how, in the middle of your own unraveling, someone else might be standing at the start of their joy.

That night, after the guests left and the dishes were stacked to dry, my mother came into my room. She sat on the edge of my bed and told me it was time for me to go to New Orleans with his family for the holidays. Said it would be "good for me"—time to bond, to rest, to prepare. But I knew better. She was passing me off. Keeping up appearances. Handing over the problem before it grew too big.

Christmas was near. They wanted me to "get to know his family better." I nodded without speaking, staring at the ceiling, wondering if God was still on the other end of my prayers. Somewhere in my chest, a quiet rebellion stirred. I didn't know it yet, but this would be the last time I felt truly powerless.

The moment I crossed that state line, something inside me whispered:
You are not safe.

And I wasn't.

Chapter 9: Spirits of New Orleans

The moment we crossed that massive bridge into the heart of New Orleans, I felt it—something ancient, something unsettled. This was post-Katrina. The city's wounds were still raw, visible in boarded windows and water-stained walls. New paint couldn't hide the bones. And I, too, was still in pieces.

The ride to his family's home was tight with silence. Zydeco blasted from the speakers—his way of filling the air without touching it. Every so often he'd ask if I was okay. I kept my eyes on the window, looking through him, not at him. My body ached—what I didn't yet know were early contractions—and my spirit felt like it was fraying thread by thread.

When we arrived, the door opened to his whole family: his parents, his twin sister who looked nothing like him, another sister with a masculine presence that filled the room. She flirted openly—called me sexy—and I laughed too quickly, unsure how else to respond. Then, as if someone flipped a switch, the entire house slid into rapid-fire Dominican Spanish. From what I caught, something had been stolen. His mother paced the house, shouting accusations into the phone. Everyone searched for the missing thing while I sat on the couch, barely breathing.

The house itself was small; two stories tucked into a weary neighborhood. Christmas decorations covered every surface—lights blinking, figurines spinning. It should have felt festive. Instead, the air felt haunted.

I was already spiritually bruised, but New Orleans scraped at something deeper. The thick air carried whispers, the ghosts of old grief curling like smoke around the edges of my thoughts. And there I was—a young girl, carrying a baby I never asked for—perched in a stranger's living room as my body quietly prepared to open.

Back in Houston, the doctors had labeled me high-risk. One even scheduled an abortion without my consent. When I realized what he was doing, I ran—screaming down sterile hallways until I collapsed in the car, demanding to be taken home. That baby was mine. Not his legacy. Not anyone's but mine.

Through everything, I clung to my Bible. Even in my darkest hours, I began to believe this child would save me. He was the reason to keep breathing, the thread keeping me alive.

Then came the dream.

A baby crying, arms outstretched, reaching for me. And just as I touched him, something dark swept in and took him away. I woke up screaming, sheets damp with sweat. I knew then: I would fight for this child with everything I had.

And then—the night it all broke open.

I couldn't move easily anymore, so when I needed to shower, I asked him for help. In a moment of pain and desperation, I asked him to touch me. I thought maybe it would numb me. Instead, it hurt worse than labor. His body felt wrong—intrusive. I hated myself for asking.

The next morning, he cooked breakfast as if nothing had happened. I sat on the phone, quietly begging my parents to come get me. They told me to wait. I hung up.

In the bathroom, I wiped and froze. Something strange—slick, unfamiliar—stained the tissue. I called him in. He told me to call my doctor in Houston. The doctor's voice was urgent:
"Go to the hospital. Now."

They wanted me to eat first. I refused. Called my parents again, demanded they drive down immediately. Eventually his mother took me to the hospital, where I sat in a wheelchair for over an hour, gripping the armrests as contractions ripped through me. My prayer was constant: *Not now. Not here. Please, God.*

When the nurse examined me, her face went pale. Seven centimeters. The baby was coming fast. They tried medication to stop it. It failed.

While I labored, his mother left for Walmart and returned with bags of baby things—clothes, bottles, a car seat. I snapped. It wasn't about the brand; it was about care. He called me bougie. I didn't care.

When my parents finally arrived, I begged everyone to leave. My father stood at the door like a soldier, letting no one in. It was just my mother, the nurses, the doctor—and me.

Three pushes. He slipped into the world. Tiny. Too early. They whisked him away and I held my breath.

No breathing machine. No defects. No visible trauma. Just a small, beautiful boy with a head full of silky hair—a child who had survived a war before his first breath.

That night, they brought him back to me. I looked into his eyes, and for the first time in years, I felt love that asked for nothing in return.

We filed the paperwork, left the father's name blank. My dad's rule: no DNA test, no claim. On the drive back to Houston, we dropped him at his apartment. I never heard from him again.

But I wasn't alone. I had my son—my tiny flame, my holy reminder that even after storms, life can return.

Chapter 10: Milk, Prayer, and Smoke

For a while, I disappeared.

I wasn't hiding—I was healing. Drifting in the soft silence that follows a storm. I stayed off social media, ignored the world, and wrapped myself in the rhythm of feedings, lullabies, and midnight cries. My arms were full, but so was my soul. I was someone's mother now. And though the ground beneath me still trembled, something sacred had begun to root itself deep within me.

Under my mother's roof, I learned how to care for my child. Not always gently. Not always joyfully. But it was her Caribbean way, and I was determined not to fail. I moved through those early days like I was balancing glass— exhausted, tender, holy. There was no manual, only instinct. No peace, only the hush of prayers whispered during nap time. I was barely nineteen, and already I felt ancient.

Eventually, I began sharing pieces of my new life—just a photo here, a baby laugh there. His big, bright eyes. His toothless smile. One post after another, and the reactions flooded in: shock, disbelief, curiosity. Old classmates, friends, and cousins I hadn't heard from in years filled my inbox.

You had a baby?

Is that YOUR son?

Their comments made me feel like I'd come back from the dead. I had vanished and reemerged not as the girl they remembered, but as someone new. A mother. A quiet warrior.

I got my first real job at CVS—stocking shelves during the day and studying college forms at night. The University of Houston surprised me by accepting me without my parents' permission. Because I had a baby, I finally qualified as independent. The irony wasn't lost on me: the very thing that had threatened to break me had opened a door no one else ever would.

I enrolled. I didn't know what I wanted to study—only that I was hungry. I walked into classrooms with bottles in my purse and a pacifier in my hoodie pocket. No time for clubs or sports. The basketball program offered me a spot, but only as a water girl. That dream had passed. My baby had replaced the ball. And yet, he gave me something even greater to run toward.

Somewhere deep down, I still hoped for my son's father to step in. I reached out first to my ex-boyfriend, the rapper. Not for me, but for my child. I thought if I reminded him of what we'd shared, he'd return—not as a lover, but as a father.

Instead, he offered me a twisted kind of love. "Islam allows it," he said, trying to convince me to become his second wife. I played along longer than I should have, telling myself I was doing it for my son. But really, I was still searching. I read the Quran while his girlfriend curled her hair. I babysat their children so they could go out. I called it faith, but really, I was being used.

It ended ugly—doors slamming, a fight with her, and me leaving for good.

But not before I met his older brother.

He was a storm in human skin—commanding, cold, wrapped in women and gold. A man of contradictions: part street prophet, part kingpin. A self-declared "gorilla pimp," though I didn't understand the weight of that title then. Surrounded by white girls he called "snow bunnies," he moved through rooms like a conductor, each woman dancing to his rhythm.

But with me, he was different. Protective, even. "You could never be pimped," he told me. "You talk too much. You think too hard. You'd ruin the game." And I believed him.

Through him, I met Paris. One of his girls, though I didn't see it that way at first. She was just a year younger than me, but carried herself like she'd lived twice the life. Heavily pregnant with one child, balancing another on her hip. Her baby boy had soft, sleepy eyes, and in time she made me his godmother. We bonded over diapers, late-night feedings, and the unspoken language young mothers share.

But there were things Paris didn't tell me—or maybe I just didn't know how to see them.

One day, she called during one of my classes. Her voice was raw, panicked. I left campus without thinking. Found her barefoot, baby carrier in one hand, blood on her face. I begged her to go to the hospital. She refused. Instead, she sat in my passenger seat in silence, ignoring call after call, before asking me to take her back to the apartment. The next day, she acted like nothing had happened.

I started noticing cracks in the mask.

One evening, I was at her apartment with the kids when her boyfriend—the "pimp"—came home drunk and angry. He exploded on all three women, shoving them, yelling. I grabbed the babies and locked us in a bedroom. I prayed until the storm passed. My heart kept pounding long after the silence returned. Before sunrise, I slipped out and didn't look back.

For weeks, I stayed away—until they invited me to a block party. "Just something casual," they said. Food, music, a few laughs. I hesitated, but curiosity tugged me back.

And it was there—in the chaos, the smoke, the bass rolling over rooftops—that I met Ron.

By then, Paris had become more than just a friend. She babysat my son while I went to class, sometimes calling between lectures just to check in. It was her, in her street-wise voice, who first told me about child support. I hadn't even thought to ask. A couple of months after dropping my son's father at his apartment for the last time, I reached out. Told him I needed help. That I was trying to get my baby into daycare so I could work and go to school.

He said he'd rather babysit himself than send his son to strangers.

I was tired. Broke.

So, I said yes.

But one day, everything shifted.

I showed up to pick up my baby, and his father met me at the door with a new kind of energy—cold, commanding, like I was no longer the mother of his child but just another girl to put in her place.

He told me I wasn't responsible enough and refused to hand my son over.

His words cut like a blade, but I wasn't leaving without my baby.

I pounded on that door until my hands ached—screaming, crying, my chest splitting open. When he finally cracked it open, I shoved my way inside, wild with panic and maternal rage. He overpowered me easily and threw me out like I was nothing.

Concrete met my knees. I stayed there, sobbing and bruised, until the police came.

It was my first arrest.

The holding cell was a box of cold air and low voices, crowded with women who all seemed to be waiting for something they couldn't name. But in the back corner, one woman sat apart—a large Black woman, rocking herself, eyes wide but far away. Something in her reminded me of my mother.

Then she began to shift. One moment a child, the next a grieving grandmother, then a teenage boy barking curses— voices and mannerisms snapping into place as if her soul was splitting into other lives. I sat frozen, unsure whether to pray for her or just bear witness.

By morning, they numbered me and sent me to county. Another cell. Another limbo. That's where I called Paris. She came with Ron, waiting for my release.

In front of the judge, I barely heard the charges. My body was there, but my spirit was still outside that apartment, screaming for my child. All I could say was, *"He took my baby."* The judge must have heard the truth in my voice because she let me go with a warning: *This isn't how you get him back.*

I nodded, but inside I was already planning. I would not give up.

There was something quiet about Ron—not soft, but still. Like a lake that hid more depth than its surface betrayed. I'd met him in a night full of chaos and noise, yet his presence cut through it like a pocket of silence in a storm.

He didn't try to impress me. He didn't perform. And after everything I'd survived, that alone made him different.

We started small—side glances, quick jokes, shared rides. I was fragile then: bruised by love, betrayal, motherhood, and the ache of being misunderstood. He didn't ask me to explain myself or to be anything other than what I was. He just kept showing up.

When Paris bailed me out, he came too. When my ex twisted the truth, Ron didn't feed the fire—he just listened. Believed me. And one day, he drove me to get my baby back himself.

It wasn't a fireworks romance. No dizzy rush. Just this slow-building peace every time he was near. For once, I wasn't being dragged into someone else's storm—I was being invited into stillness.

Spiritually, I was split—half tethered to the scriptures I'd grown up with, half drifting in the chaos I was living. But Ron made me feel like maybe God could be found in the quiet. In the healing. In the being.

Moving in together felt less like a decision and more like something inevitable. We found an apartment near Paris—close enough for comfort, far enough to try to build something of our own.

Then came the crack in the foundation.

Not long after we unpacked, Ron told me he had just come home from a seven-year bid. Domestic violence. Against the mother of his children. His voice was low, careful—like he knew the weight of those words might make me run. But I didn't. I was already in too deep. Maybe too accustomed to surviving chaos to fear it. I thought I could love him into peace.

He began showing me pieces of his world—how he'd survived inside: prison food alchemy, turning ramen, chips, pickles, and hot sauce into something he called "ghetto dope." He blasted old-school tracks I'd never heard, until they became the soundtrack of that apartment. I helped catalog his artwork and flash books, even sold his mixtapes.

He wrote poetry, too—long, looping verses in a perfect cursive that looked more like art than words. There was brilliance in him, no doubt.

But there was also something else.

Something dark.

At first, it was small things—odd whispers in the night, a chill that settled in our bedroom without warning. Then he started talking about magic. Not just metaphorical magic— the real kind. He told me there was "white magic" and "black magic," and that he only worked with white. I didn't know what to make of it, so I tried to laugh it off, tried to stay open. But then he told me he had opened a portal in our closet. That I wasn't allowed in there. Ever.

I obeyed. But I started feeling things.

There were nights I couldn't sleep. Shadows moved on their own. I heard voices I couldn't trace. The air in that apartment got heavier by the day, especially near that closet. It wasn't just fear—it was knowing. My spirit knew what my mind tried to ignore. I would sit on the couch, holding my baby tighter than usual, eyes darting toward that door. Ron said I was just sensitive, but I knew what I felt. Something had entered our home. Something unwelcome.

It didn't help that our apartment sat next to a cemetery. Literally. I could look out the window and see gravestones lining up like soldiers guarding the dead. At first, it felt poetic. Now it just felt like an omen.

I wanted to believe Ron was only exploring another way to heal. I wanted to believe his magic was harmless. But my soul told me otherwise. And that still, quiet peace he once brought into my life? It began to dissolve into something else—something unsettling.

He was a tattoo artist with a kind of genius I had never seen. I'd sit on the bed, rocking my son, and watch him work—taking blank skin and turning it into something holy, chaotic, eternal. His drawings were never just one thing. He layered images like memories—ghosts overlapping blessings, pain threaded through beauty. One picture over another, and another, until the entire page became a mural of every lifetime he had lived. And somehow, he managed to do it on skin too. It fascinated me. It took months for me to convince him to give me my first tattoo. He drew my face with a rose and a tear before the storm came.

A hurricane swept through Houston like it had a score to settle—fast, violent, unforgiving. It ripped through our complex with a rage I'd only ever felt inside my chest. A patio chair flew through our apartment window like a warning. The lights went out, the silence that followed wasn't peace—it was survival. My neighbor, whose family owned a meat market, pulled out a steel pit in the middle of the courtyard and started barbecuing everything before it could spoil. For a moment, there was a strange kind of unity. Kids played in the rainwater. We all shared what little we had. But that stillness didn't last. Then came the food drops—military bags left on curbs like rations in a war zone. The danger didn't just come from nature—it came from people, hungry and desperate. That's when I made the hardest call: I brought my baby back to my mother's house. Just until I could figure things out. Just until I found a way to keep him safe.

And then Ron came to me with a plan, or at least a promise. He said he had family in Detroit, that they could help us get a fresh start. He swore we would come back for my son. I didn't want to go. Every fiber of my being screamed to stay. But I was tired. Spiritually worn. And I wanted to believe that something better was waiting. When it came time to catch the Greyhound, I hesitated. My chest ached. My hands trembled. That's when he handed me a little yellow pill, something he called a "school bus." I swallowed it without thinking. My next memory was waking up in Detroit, far from home, far from my son, with no clear path back.

Detroit was unlike anything I'd ever seen. It felt like stepping through a tear in time—like I had wandered into the soul of a 1970s postcard no one dared send. As we neared downtown, I watched black men strut past neon-lit bars in vibrant suits, wide-brimmed hats, and polished shoes. Some carried canes, not out of necessity but as declarations of pride. The street pulsed with music and memory. But I wasn't there to dance—I was a ghost floating beside Ron, unsure of how I got there. He took me to a run-down motel, the kind that hums with the secrets of a hundred broken stories. The room was dim and worn, with cigarette burns on the sheets and spirits lingering in the corners. I was afraid to leave. The neighborhood whispered danger with every step, so I stayed behind while he left. When he returned, he was different. Quiet. Focused. He told me he had picked up "an eight ball," but I didn't ask what that meant. I didn't want to know. He unpacked his tools and ink, started working on tattoos by lamplight while I helped organize pages of lyrics, old notebooks, and crumpled CD covers. His dreams were still alive, loud and chaotic like the beats coming from the street outside. He believed he could sell his songs to DJs at the bars nearby. He moved in and out of the room like a shadow—disappearing, then returning with money, food, or silence. I waited. That's all I could do. Then one day, he looked up and said, "Nashville. I gotta make a stop before we go back to Houston." And I went with him. Because I didn't know how to say no. Because part of me still believed we were on our way back home.

We landed in Nashville—or as everyone around us called it, *Cashville, Ten A Key*. The name itself rang with promise, but it carried the weight of something else too. We checked into another roadside motel near downtown. This one felt different. The air didn't choke me. The sky opened a little wider. Maybe God was giving me space to think, to feel again. Ron stepped out more often, and for once, I wasn't afraid to do the same. He even encouraged me—told me to go meet people. I didn't understand it at the time, but now I know: he was releasing me in his own way.

But just as I began to taste that freedom, the cord snapped. One afternoon, he returned with two girls I didn't know. I watched in horror and heartbreak as he used them right in front of me—like I was invisible. My heart screamed silently. I thought I loved him. I thought what we shared meant something sacred. But he looked through me and said I was too young to be his wife. That night, I didn't sleep. Something in me shattered, and something else began to awaken.

So I left. I wandered into the heart of downtown and found myself in a three-story club glowing like a cathedral of sound. The music wrapped around me like a prayer I didn't know I needed. I danced until I forgot my name. That's where I met Matthew. An older white man, crisp button-down, jeans, and a leather jacket. He had gentle eyes and a stillness about him, like maybe he'd walked through storms too. He offered me a drink and a moment of ease. We danced, laughed, and exchanged numbers. He didn't want anything from me—just my presence. And in that brief exchange, I felt seen, like the universe was whispering, *You're not lost. You're just becoming.*

Soon after, we packed up again. This time, to St. Louis. But part of me stayed in Nashville—in that glowing club, on that floor where my soul stirred awake.

St. Louis looked just as forgotten as Detroit—weathered buildings, cracked sidewalks, and a heaviness in the air that made it hard to breathe. We found another motel across from a mall, and for a moment I thought maybe this time would be different. But hope faded fast. He brought me to a house that looked like it had survived too many storms—windows boarded up, walls buckling with secrets. I didn't want to stay. It felt wrong. Like something holy had been stripped from the foundation. That's when I met *him*—a man they said was sick, dying of cancer, but with a surplus of pills that could keep others on their feet or knock them off entirely. It wasn't long before a suitcase filled with those pills became my burden to carry. My hands, once cradling a baby, now gripped plastic bottles with names I couldn't pronounce.

Then the chaos cracked wide open. Ron got arrested while driving with that man—just vanished from my side like a ghost sucked back into the prison system he never really left. He left me behind in that motel, sitting on a stained bed, surrounded by narcotics and confusion. I didn't know what I was holding. I didn't know if someone was coming to take it back. All I knew was that I was alone. Again. I tried to bond him out, desperate to find ground beneath me, but they told me he had a warrant. He was being extradited back to Houston. A free ride home for him. A deeper exile for me. I gathered everything I could, left some behind, put money on his books, and walked into the Greyhound station with shaking hands. I bought a ticket back to Houston—back to my son, back to my storm—but this time, something inside me had changed. I didn't yet know the name for it. Maybe it was courage. Maybe it was surrender.

The bus out of St. Louis was supposed to bring me home— to my son, to something familiar. Instead, it steered me deeper into a maze of wrong turns and silent prayers. I found a seat next to a white guy who called himself *Ghost*. Baggy jeans, one earring, headphones bleeding rap so loud I could feel the bass from my side of the seat. I told him I rapped too, and something clicked. For hours we freestyled, tossing rhymes back and forth like they were currency. We laughed. We vibed. The miles melted.

Then at one stop, he vanished. And so did my wallet.

Panic flared up in my chest. I asked the bus driver where he went. "Florida," she said like it was the next town over.

Without thinking, I bought another ticket—this time to Florida—praying I'd find him. And somehow, I did. Ghost reappeared like he never left, handed me my wallet— empty—and then disappeared again, this time for good. I was stunned, stranded, and spiraling in the wrong direction.

When I finally reached New Orleans again, something felt off. As the bus pulled into the terminal, dogs waited outside. Drug dogs. My pulse raced. I didn't know exactly what I had anymore, only that I shouldn't have had it. In a panic, I shoved everyone around me and ran into the giant station lobby. That's when the bus driver found me again—looked me in the eyes like she'd seen girls like me before—and simply said, "Take the train. It's safer." So I did. And it was. Safer, yes. But longer. Four hours stretched into ten.

During that endless ride, I met a white woman—loud, brash, and unapologetic. She was heading to Houston to meet her husband, a construction worker staying in a motel near the old Reliant Stadium We talked. Too much. Somehow, I admitted I had pills. Maybe I was tired of hiding. Maybe I wanted someone to tell me what to do. Her eyes lit up, not with concern, but curiosity.

I didn't trust her. But fate, or something like it, brought her back into my life just hours later.

I finally made it to Houston, dragging my weary body to my mother's house. I thought maybe she'd see the exhaustion in my eyes. But she didn't see me at all. We argued. She screamed. She kicked me out.

I stood outside, alone again, with nowhere to go.

So I called the woman from the train.

She came quickly, took me to the motel. The room was thick with smoke, laughter, and bodies. Everyone was partying like the world had already ended. I sat in the corner, too hollow to move. Sleep took me like a thief.

The next thing I remember was chaos.

Police stormed the room. Voices yelling. Hands grabbing. Lights flashing.

And then: handcuffs.

I was arrested. Again.

This time, they didn't stop at holding cells or booking. They took me straight downtown—into the heart of Houston's jail system. The air inside was cold, metallic, and thick with the scent of despair. I was led down sterile corridors and placed into a concrete cell with a group of other young women. Each face told its own story: some hardened, some haunted, some hollow. Prostitution, drug charges, assault, even murder—these were the lives swirling around me now. I didn't know what my charge was. I didn't ask. I kept quiet, head down, spirit aching.

I knew enough by now to keep my mouth shut. Jail wasn't the place for explanations or tears. It was a different world with its own language, its own rules. If I was going to survive in there, I had to make friends—and fast. So I listened. I observed. I folded into the rhythm of the place: concrete benches for beds, stale food served on color-coded trays, fluorescent lights that never went out. The jail was a warehouse for forgotten souls—brick by brick built to erase you.

When the phones finally buzzed on, I lined up like everyone else. There was only one person I trusted to answer—Paris. By now, she had left my so-called "brother-in-law" and was settling with someone new, someone I later realized was another pimp wearing a different face. Still, she picked up. I gave her Matthew's number and begged her to call him on three-way. When his voice finally came through the static, something in me cracked open.

I poured out everything. My mother had kicked me out. She had taken my baby. I had been roaming city to city with pills I couldn't even name, arrested and thrown in a cage for crimes I didn't fully understand. I was tired—tired of the running, the chasing, the pretending I was okay. I told Matthew everything, raw and unfiltered, and the silence on the other end told me he heard me.

Days later, the impossible happened.

My name was called.

I braced for court, for shackles, for judgment. But instead, they handed me my things and opened the door. No judge. No explanation. No paperwork. Just freedom.

To this day, I don't know who pulled the strings. But I felt it deep in my spirit—God had stepped in. Not because I deserved it. But because He wasn't finished with me yet.

And as I stepped out into the sunlight, blinking like a newborn, I made a vow: *I'm not going back.*

Paris picked me up like a vision out of a movie—heels clicking, lashes long, looking like she'd stepped off a screen or maybe a stage. She looked so polished, so unfazed, I almost forgot we came from the same chaos. But I saw it in her eyes. Stillness on the surface. Storm underneath.

It had been months. I didn't know what I expected. She took me back to her new apartment, where three other girls moved like shadows with names I don't remember—only tones, accents, vibes. Two were light-skinned, Southern and soft-spoken, like they hadn't figured out this world yet. The third was white, chubby, dressed in baggy clothes with a DJ's confidence and a record label hustle. Everyone played a part. Everyone followed unspoken rules. I just didn't know mine yet.

Then one night, everything changed.

The door creaked open. And there *he* was. The Pimp.

Nobody had told him I was staying there. I could tell the moment his eyes landed on me—I wasn't supposed to be there. His stare was cold. Not confusion. Not curiosity. Just calculation. My breath caught in my chest. Paris moved quickly, grabbed his hand, and whispered something. Then they disappeared into the back room.

She didn't come out until morning.

She was bruised. But smiling. Like nothing happened. Like she'd practiced this kind of forgetting.

"We're going out tonight," she said, like it was normal. Then came the warning:

"We can't come back until we've made a thousand dollars."

She said it so casually. Like a chore. Like a dare. Then she said we were going shopping.

We drove to Hilcroft—rows of discount boutiques and quick fashion. She handed me clothes I wouldn't have picked for myself—tight, racy, loud. Armor for the night ahead. We returned to the apartment, got dressed, picked up the other girls, and headed out.

Until that night, I had never *been* part of this. I had watched it from the edges. But now I was in the car, heels strapped on, lip gloss shining, laughing at jokes that weren't funny because I was scared to death.

Initially, she tried to get me hired at a strip club that one of the girls preformed at, but they refused since I couldn't pole dance to save my life and then we club-hopped like stars on tour. Flashing lights, men throwing cash, music so loud it drowned out my thoughts. We danced. We drank. We played the part. And I'll be honest—*some of it felt freeing.* Like I could be someone else for just one night. But freedom built on fear is a lie. And that lie started unraveling fast.

Because when the night ended... we didn't go home.

We pulled into a dark apartment complex. The engine idled. Paris turned to me and said, "Wait here." Then she hopped out of the car and vanished into the shadows.

She came back not long after—hair messed, lipstick smudged, eyes glowing like she just beat a level in a dangerous game. "Let's go," she said. No one asked questions.

Next stop: the motel. The two younger girls exchanged nervous glances. They got out of the car and walked toward the room like they were walking a plank. Less than twenty minutes later, they came sprinting back—hair flying, shoes in hand. Paris hit the gas. We sped off into the dark.

Eventually, the storm in me demanded answers.

I turned to Paris, my voice trembling under the weight of what I needed to know.

"What did you do in that room?"

She hesitated—laughed nervously, brushed it off like I was just being naïve. But I wasn't letting it go. I asked again. Then again. Until she finally surrendered and laid it all out, step by step. Like it was normal. Like this was just how you survived when the world stopped caring.

Her words carved something open in me. She spoke like it was easy—like the human heart could be silenced with enough practice. But I felt everything. I couldn't understand how she let someone touch her like that... how she gave away the pieces of herself like they weren't sacred. I wasn't judging her—I was just heartbroken. For her. For us. For the way the world warped women into shapes we were never meant to take.

My anger came rushing out—not at her, but at the brokenness we were drowning in.

So, I made a decision.

The next time we rolled up, I looked her in the eyes and said, "When you go in…take this, knock them out. Then I'll come."

She blinked, then smiled—like I'd finally graduated.

We made a plan, she called it "two-girl special." She went in first, charmed them, played the part. If they said yes, she'd send the signal. I'd follow with the ecstasy and the plan. We laughed. We flirted. We waited for them to fold under the poison, and when they did, we ran—pockets full, spirits empty.

We did this for days. We moved like ghosts. Always high. Always pretending.

And for a moment, I felt powerful—like I'd outsmarted the world that kept trying to take me. But deep down, I knew I was breaking. I was silencing my own soul just to hear something louder than the loneliness.

Then it happened.

One night in the club. The bass thumping. The lights spinning. The air thick with perfume and sweat and danger. Paris locked eyes with someone across the room and her entire body stiffened.

It was him.

Her old pimp. My so-called brother-in-law. The one she swore she'd escaped. The one we both feared more than we ever admitted.

She turned and bolted for the car. I was right behind her.

But before she could drive off, he was already there. He *dragged* her out of the window like she was nothing.

I hid behind another car, watching, shaking, my hands over my mouth. She was screaming. Fighting. Kicking. But it didn't matter.

He had her.

And they left me there—alone in a parking lot, high out of my mind, heart cracking in places I didn't know existed.

In that moment, I realized:

This wasn't a movie.

This wasn't a game.

This was survival. And I had to decide who I was going to be.

I was done pretending I could dance through hell and not get burned. The spirits had been warning me for a while, but now I heard them loud and clear.

I was in over my head.

And it was time to choose—fight for my soul or let it disappear.

The rest of that night plays back in fragments. Lights. Music. Movement. After Paris was dragged away, I was paralyzed in that parking lot, stuck between flight and collapse. Then, like an answered prayer in the form of distraction, I found the twins—two brothers I had danced with earlier, carefree and full of rhythm. They reminded me of something that felt safe. Normal. Like home.

I clung to them, begged them to take me somewhere—
anywhere—but back into that madness. They didn't ask
questions. Just nodded. We ended up at their apartment,
somewhere near the Reliant Stadium again. That place had
become a strange orbit for me—where chaos always circled
close but never quite landed the same way twice.

The twins weren't like the others. They had kids—five or six
between them—and real jobs that kept them grounded. They
danced, yes, but for money at clubs on the weekends, doing
synchronized routines that were more art than hustle. They
were kind. Quiet. And when they saw the look in my eyes,
the silence in my spirit, they gave me space. They offered
shelter, not judgment.

One of them let me borrow his laptop. I sat on the couch for
hours, trying to piece my life back together. Searching for
answers. For direction. For *myself.* I had nothing—no ID, no
money, no plan. Just a heart that wouldn't die, no matter how
many times it broke.

Then came the fire.

It ripped through the apartment complex, forcing everyone
out. The heat, the sirens, the screaming—it felt metaphorical,

like the final unraveling of a version of me I could no longer return to. I fled barefoot, clutching the few clothes I had, unsure of what was next.

And that's when I found my sister.

She lived nearby, also off the stadium loop, and though I hadn't seen her in months, she opened the door. I didn't tell her everything. I couldn't. But the worry in her eyes was enough to say she knew. She scolded me like a mother would. Told me to get it together. That I needed to fight for my son.

And she was right. But I didn't know how. I was still so broken. So, lost.

Then I remembered Matthew.

I had forgotten to even tell him I was free. I called him and when he answered, it was like a lifeline snapped back into place. I gave him just enough of the story to understand— and that's when he made the promise.

"If you come back to Nashville," he said, "I'll help you. I'll get you a place. A car. A fresh start."

I didn't say yes right away. My heart tugged in too many directions. I missed my son like oxygen. But my mother refused to hand him over. Word had gotten around—rumors from cousins who'd seen me in the clubs. I could hear the judgment in her voice even when she said nothing.

Still, I made a vow to myself.

Get stable. Get strong. Then go back and get him.

So, I packed what little I had left.

And I left—again.

But this time, I prayed the leaving would lead me back to healing.

Chapter 11: False Comforts and Digital Doorways

I didn't take the Greyhound to Nashville—I flew. One-way ticket. No return plan. The moment the wheels left the ground, it felt like releasing a breath I didn't realize I'd been holding for months. For the first time in what felt like forever, I wasn't looking over my shoulder. I was moving toward something, chasing a promise—Matthew's promise.

He was waiting for me at the airport, the kind of entrance that could've belonged to a film: polished shoes, warm smile, leather jacket. For a split second, I let myself believe I was being rescued.

This time, he didn't take me to the streets. He took me to a Marriott—clean, quiet, with white sheets that smelled faintly of bleach and comfort. Real room service. For two weeks, I lived in a bubble of borrowed peace. I ate full meals. Took showers without locking the door. Slept without jerking awake to every sound. I'd sit on the bed, watching the TV on mute, just grateful for the silence. I started journaling again, my handwriting shaky but steadying. I prayed again. Slowly, I began to remember pieces of myself I thought I'd lost.

But peace, I would learn, doesn't always mean truth.

The truth came like a pin to a balloon—quiet, quick, and devastating. Matthew was married. Not separated. Married.

The news didn't break me because I loved him—I didn't. It broke me because I'd wanted to believe someone had come for me without conditions or hidden chains. I wanted to believe I had been chosen. But in that instant, the illusion shattered. I looked around the hotel room and saw it differently—not a sanctuary, but a beautiful cage.

That ache—the hollow hunger to belong—pulled me back into the digital world. Social media became my escape hatch once more. I made a profile on MocoSpace, and just like that, the floodgates opened.

That's where I met Trevor.

And Chris.

Chapter 12: Divine Distraction

Trevor pulled up in a sleek BMW, tinted windows rolling down like a scene ripped from a music video. He flashed a grin—clean-cut, smooth, his confidence teetering just shy of cocky. I climbed in, still emotionally raw but willing to believe in something light, even if only for a moment. I needed light.

His place was on the TSU campus, but there was a twist—Trevor didn't just have one apartment. He had two. Side by side. One was spotless, private, almost curated. The other was alive—laughter spilling out the door, music vibrating through the walls, and about eight of the finest men I'd ever seen inside: football players, a local DJ everyone seemed to know by name. The air pulsed like a living thing, and when I walked in, every eye locked on me.

They thought I was the entertainment.

I laughed it off, played along—flirting, teasing, hiding my unease beneath practiced charm. But then the air shifted. The music cut. One of them stepped forward and asked, straight-faced, "So… which one of us you picking?"

I froze for half a beat, then smiled and leaned toward the safest choice. "I'm with Trevor."

He nodded like he already knew, then called for more girls—college friends, party regulars, energy to fill the room. Me and Trevor slipped away to his private apartment, leaving behind the testosterone and tension.

That night, we talked. Not surface talk—the kind that reaches under your guard. He told jokes sharp enough to crack the heavy shell I'd been carrying. I laughed in a way I hadn't in months. He reminded me of the boys I might have dated if life had been gentler—the ones who held doors open and made you feel beautiful without laying a hand on you. He had a rhythm, a magnetic ease, and when I told him he could be a comedian, I meant it. His gift was pulling the sadness out of me and replacing it with something lighter.

We woke together the next morning like it was nothing—no pressure, no shame. Just two souls who'd needed warmth. And he kept showing up. Daily. Picking me up. Taking me out to eat. Parties. Laughter. Healing, disguised as simplicity.

Trevor wasn't my forever, but he was a soft place to land. A pause between storms. I wasn't chasing love anymore. I was searching for connection—a place to set my loneliness down.

Then came Chris.

He was the first white wannabe gangster I'd ever met. Baggy jeans sagging enough to flash his boxers, a gold chain swinging like it was an extension of his swagger. He typed in a language of misspelled slang and emojis, like he'd been raised in the back of a Lil Wayne music video. But he made me laugh—really laugh. And strangely, he made me feel seen.

There was a wildness in him I recognized—the kind I'd grown up around. Boys with trauma buried under bravado, weed smoke, and jokes. Chris talked fast, lived faster, and within days he'd invited me into his world—a wooden deck, a hot tub steaming under the Tennessee sky, loud music spilling from a small county house. He was supposed to be in high school, but school was already a closed chapter to him.

The house was always full—two guys he called cousins, and Sarah, a girl who always looked too nervous for her age. I later learned she was a runaway, younger than she claimed.

Chris was the reason I stayed in Nashville. His family owned a farm, but their cash crop was something else entirely—weed. At first, I only knew it by smell and the occasional hit at a party. But Chris, with his chaotic enthusiasm, taught me everything. He had a closet grow system, purple lights humming like a secret blooming in the dark. I watered plants, trimmed leaves, nurtured them like they were something pure. With my new college connections and party crowd, I sold every ounce.

It felt too easy.

The money came fast. The attention, faster. For a brief moment, I felt powerful again. Not in control, but close as if I was rebuilding something from the dirt.

Then Matthew showed up.

Chris saw him and something in his face hardened. His voice sharpened, deepened. Without warning, he told me to get out. No reason. No conversation. Just rage, like I had crossed a line I hadn't known existed.

And just like that, I was homeless again.

I refused to go back to Chris's. I begged Matthew to drop me somewhere—anywhere—to catch my breath. We found a roadside motel, the kind with doors opening straight onto the parking lot and a neon sign buzzing like a warning. I told myself I'd only be there a night or two.

I still had clothes, my suitcase—things at Chris's place. Sarah, bless her, snuck them out for me and brought them to the motel. She stayed too. Maybe out of loyalty. Maybe fear. Maybe both. Two girls playing grown in a world that swallowed girls like us whole.

Then he came.

Not invited. Not known to us. Just a shadow at first—a drug dealer from the parking lot who must have smelled the vulnerability. He walked in like he owned the place, dropped his stash on the table, and started selling right there. Like we were furniture. Like we didn't matter.

Sarah panicked and ran—back to Chris's, back to whatever felt safer than this. I stayed. Alone.

I begged the front desk to move me to another room. Too late. He found me again.

God, Are You Listening?

This time, he didn't knock. He stepped inside, cornered me. His words were low, deliberate. I knew what was coming— the tone, the posture, the silence between threats. He told me he'd have his way with me. Like it was his right.

I prayed.

Not with words—just tears. A silent scream I sent to heaven.

And then, a miracle.

His phone rang.

His baby mama.

And just like that, he left.

He stormed out cussing, but he left.

The silence that followed was so loud it made my ears ring. I stood there shaking, wondering if I'd imagined it all, wondering if I was safe—or just standing in the eye of the storm.

I grabbed my phone and started texting anyone whose name I could scroll to. I didn't care who. I just needed someone to come. To save me. To see me. Chris ignored me. Trevor actually responded—said he was on his way—but he never made it. Later, he told me he'd been pulled over for a DUI that night.

And then there was David.

The last person I expected. The only one who came.

He arrived like a storm wrapped in silk—swagger stitched into every step, the kind of Brooklyn confidence that could fill a room without ever raising its voice. He looked at me like he'd already read my story cover to cover. And then, without hesitation, he claimed me: "You mine now. I'm gonna protect you. You don't have to live like this no more."

I wanted to believe him. God, I needed to believe *someone.*

He didn't take me far—just down the street—but it might as well have been another world. The apartment reeked of cigarette smoke, weed, and the kind of funk that lives in old carpet and never leaves. A circle of men lounged inside— one in a wheelchair, others shirtless, gold teeth flashing as they laughed over liquor bottles. It was chaos, but it had a strange warmth. Not safe, but familiar. David called them *family.*

And just like that, I became his shadow.

David carried a current with him. Wherever he went, people seemed to light up. He didn't just walk into a room—he became the rhythm of it. Women adored him. Men respected him. Kids gravitated toward him. When he introduced me— *"This here's my girl"*—there was pride in his voice, like I belonged there.

For the first time in a long time, I felt seen.

His world unfolded around me. Aunts, uncles, cousins, friends who treated him like blood. They welcomed me with jokes, hugs, and plates of food. Inside their mess and madness was a glimpse of something I had always craved: family that didn't question how you got there, family that simply made room for you.

I knew it was fragile. I knew it wasn't the fairy tale. But after everything I'd been through, it was enough. I clung to it like a lifeline. Because sometimes, even a broken family can feel like salvation.

It didn't take long for the picture to sharpen—David was a Blood. The men in that rundown apartment weren't just friends; they were soldiers. Red bandanas, coded words, movements in sync like a trained unit. It scared me at first. But fear had been my shadow for so long, it almost felt like comfort. And more than anything, I wanted to matter to something.

What surprised me most wasn't the violence—they tried to shield me from that—it was the art. These same men who lived by the block carried music in their bones. Beats. Bars. Rhymes. It burned in them like fire.

And so did I.

With scraps of experience from past studios and late-night freestyles, I helped turn that fire into form. We got our own place—barely furnished but brimming with hope. In the corner, we built a studio: mic stand rigged from wire hangers, foam on the walls, a battered laptop looping beats into the night. We were broke but inspired, hungry in the way only dreamers can be.

The mixtapes came first—raw, relentless, pressed by hand, track by track, like we were carving our names into stone. Then came T-shirts, our story printed in bold letters like armor. A street team seemed to appear by divine timing— passing flyers like scripture, turning alleyways into revival grounds. We weren't just promoting—we were prophesying. Every verse was a prayer. Every beat, a war drum. The stage became our sanctuary. Clubs turned into cathedrals. When the crowd roared, it was like heaven cracked open just for us.

It was chaotic. Unruly. Drenched in shadow. But it was ours. And for the first time in years, I wasn't just surviving—I was creating. Breathing life into something bigger than my pain. My studio wasn't just a room; it was prophecy. A whisper from the Most High saying, *You were made to build.*

When I stepped off the plane in Houston, I promised myself this would be different. I wasn't the same girl who once ran through the streets hunting for safety. I had my own keys now. My own place. My own peace—almost. All I needed was my son to make it whole.

I walked into my parents' house like a soldier returning from war. My heart pounded, my nerves were frayed, but my resolve was solid. I wasn't there to argue or beg. I was there to take back what never should have been taken from me.

My father was there. That should have meant safety. Instead, it felt like the universe was setting me up. I moved quickly, gathering my baby's bottles, blankets, onesies—pieces of my shattered heart.

Then came the storm. My mother.

Her presence hit like thunder—loud, violent, unavoidable. Her rage rose like a tidal wave, and I was right in its path. I tried to push past her, clutching my son, but the screams started—accusations so thick they seemed to coat the air.

I ran. Down the stairs. Out of the chaos.

And at the bottom, my father stepped in front of me. Without a word, he ripped the carrier from my arms and shoved me out the door.

Just like that—the man who had once promised to protect me.

I don't know how long I sat on that sidewalk. It felt like the world had stopped spinning, like my body was outside but my soul was still in that house—screaming.

Then the cops arrived. Someone must've heard everything. I saw the flashing lights through my tears and ran to them like they were salvation. I begged, pleaded—*please just let me take my baby*. I wasn't hysterical. I was broken. Calm but unraveling. They looked at me like I was crazy.

And then he came.

My son's father. Like a ghost. Quiet. Cold. I hadn't seen him in months. He didn't look at me. Didn't speak to me. Just walked past, into the house, and then came back out... holding my son. *Our* son. He turned his back and walked away like I didn't exist.

I wanted to scream but nothing came out. I just watched them disappear. My knees hit the pavement and I collapsed.

And if that wasn't enough—my mother went to the police and poured her poison into their ears. Called me a prostitute. A criminal. A danger to my own child. I could barely process what was happening before they were putting me in handcuffs.

Turns out, someone had been arrested using my ID. A motel, a mix-up, a memory I never asked for. But none of that mattered. They took me anyway.

I sat in that Fort Bend County jail for a week. Not as a daughter. Not as a mother. Not as a human being. Just a number. Just an echo.

And when they moved me to Houston and realized the mistake, they let me go like it was nothing. Like the pieces of my soul weren't still scattered on that sidewalk.

That moment—it didn't just break me. It hollowed me. It was the worst pain I'd ever known. Not just losing my son— but being treated like I didn't deserve him. Like I wasn't real. Like love and sacrifice and pain meant nothing.

But something in that hollow place began to stir. Not anger. Not revenge. Something quieter. Deeper. A knowing. That *God still saw me.* That I wasn't forgotten. That the war wasn't over.

I left with nothing. But I was not done.

In that season, I began to see the woman buried beneath the trauma. A creator. A messenger. A voice the streets couldn't drown. A leader not born of ease, but of fire.

The foundation may have been cracked. But it held. And from it, something sacred rose.

Three months in, we were engaged. It wasn't a fairytale proposal—it was a soul contract sealed with urgency. A promise between two wounded spirits who had survived too much alone and were now choosing to walk the fire together. In a world that kept trying to break us, this felt like rebellion. A quiet, radical act of building something sacred from ash.

But then came the call. My father's voice, sharp as shattered glass: "Change your last name. You don't carry mine no more." His words didn't just cut—they buried themselves. Not just in my ears, but deep in my bones. I stood there afterward, the silence around me swelling, knowing I had finally been cast out of the lineage I once prayed would save me.

That night, I cried not because I was disowned, but because part of me had still hoped—still longed for my father's blessing. Instead, I received rejection wrapped in tradition.

Six months in, I drew a line in the spiritual sand. I looked at David and said, "Either we do this before God or we let this go." There was no anger in my voice—just clarity. Stillness. The kind that comes when you finally know your worth.

He didn't hesitate. He took me by the hand, and we walked into the courthouse like pilgrims. We didn't need witnesses—we had our ancestors. We didn't need rings—we had the fire of commitment etched into our palms from everything we'd already endured.

But David wanted more. He wanted to bless it. Sanctify it.

That night, still in the clothes we had danced in, he led me to a pastor's home. His living room had been transformed into something holy. Candles flickered with quiet reverence. A worn Bible rested open like a doorway. He built an altar with his own hands. Not from gold, but from intention.

And it was there, standing in that ordinary room made sacred by love and desperation, that I vowed with trembling lips and tear-stained cheeks. I didn't just say "I do"—I whispered a prayer through those words. A prayer that this union would redeem me. That love could be strong enough to write a new legacy, even if I had been cast out of the old one.

In that moment, I wasn't just becoming a wife—I was stepping into covenant. Not just with him, but with the woman I was destined to become. She wasn't perfect. But she was present. And finally, she was chosen.

The moment we said "I do," it was like something shifted in him—like a veil was lifted, revealing not just the man I loved, but the weight of all the power he thought marriage gave him. It wasn't gentle anymore. It wasn't sacred. It was domination dressed up as devotion.

The ring on my finger became more like a tether around my soul. At first, it was subtle—suggestions disguised as love. "Let's spice things up," he'd say, and somehow, I was convinced to share sacred space with strangers, all under the illusion of freedom. We even had a "girlfriend" for a while. It felt like a performance of love instead of the real thing, and slowly, the room that was once filled with dreams became dark with control.

Chapter 13: The Mall, the Memory, and the Casino Below

After Houston—after the truth was ripped from my hands and rewritten into something I didn't recognize—I couldn't give up. Something in me refused. I couldn't accept that my son had been swallowed by a system built on silence and betrayal.

I found him in New Orleans, living in his grandmother's house. Seeing him again was like finding a missing piece of my heart. I reached out carefully, knowing one wrong move could close the door for good. His grandmother, cautious but willing, agreed to meet.

So David and I flew to New Orleans. At the mall, we met his grandmother and aunt. For a moment, it felt almost normal—a family reunion, fragile but real. We took pictures. Proof that I had held my son again. I smiled for every photo, even while my spirit trembled. I promised I'd be back for his birthday in December and left a deposit for the celebration. I was trying—desperately—to build something back.

Then the violence came. Swift. Explosive. David could turn on a dime—charming one moment, breaking things the next. The hands that once held me became weapons. And just like that, he was gone—arrested. Locked away. I stood outside, married and more alone than I had ever been.

In that hollow space, I reached for the one person I swore I wouldn't—Matthew.
We'd kept in touch. Small check-ins. Music. Laughter. He never knew the truth of my marriage. He only knew the version I let him see: that I had a husband now, and I was "doing okay."

But   I   wasn't   okay.
I called him, voice steady but breaking. "I need help. Twelve hundred. I need to bond him out... he has to make the next show."
Silence. Then a sigh. "Okay."

I didn't tell him I was bruised. I didn't tell him that the altar I stood at had turned into a battlefield. I just needed to survive the next performance.

But deep down, I knew—no stage, no spotlight, no song could save what had already begun to shatter.

While David sat in jail making soft promises through steel bars, I found myself in Matthew's arms. Maybe it was comfort. Maybe rebellion. Maybe the last flicker of a girl who wanted to feel safe again. But it happened. And I knew the threads holding my life together were fraying fast.

David came home with the storm still in him. His apologies sounded sweet, but his eyes—those eyes—held control, anger, and something I couldn't name. I wanted to believe him. I needed to. Because right then, my world was falling apart.

Then   came   the   blow—my   son   was   gone.
No warning. No court date I could attend. Just a quiet conversation, a legal order buried under silence, and a decision already made. The court had given his father primary custody... on the grounds of abandonment. That word—*abandonment*—cut deeper than any bruise. My own mother had received the papers and said nothing. Let it happen. Let me walk blind into the loss.

Panic became purpose. I found a lawyer in Houston. She filed a motion to fight the order. I flew home—new husband in tow—clinging to hope like it was oxygen. But courtrooms aren't built for hope. They're built for war.

And my son's father came armed. He laid out David's criminal history for the judge in black and white. Violence. Rage. Records I never knew existed. My lawyer had no counterattack. The gavel might as well have been a gunshot.

That night in the hotel, I read the records. Page after page of darkness I didn't know I was living with. David's past wasn't just checkered—it was a warning I had ignored. He told me not to worry. That we'd fix everything.

But in my gut, I knew—some things can't be fixed.

Chapter 14: The Night the Waters Rose

It was supposed to be a normal night. David and I had just come home to the tiny apartment that cradled our beginnings. But the moment we stepped inside, something felt wrong.

The floor was soaked. The air clung to us with the heavy smell of mildew and something sharper—chemical, metallic. Water crept across the linoleum like a quiet warning.

It wasn't a busted pipe. It wasn't a broken appliance. It was a message.

Word had spread: David's red bandana, his blood ties, didn't sit well in a building run by MS-13. And they wanted us gone.

We were still trying to salvage the waterlogged scraps of our life when they came—men we didn't know, faces masked, weapons drawn. The parking lot thickened with danger until it felt like the air itself was holding its breath.

David called his people. They answered—two Suburbans deep, heavy with bodies and rage. I don't remember who threw the first punch. Maybe no one does. But fists flew. Bottles shattered. Shouts cut into screams.

I stood frozen, watching war explode over a patch of concrete. My heart pounded like war drums in my chest. Then someone grabbed me, yanking me into a Suburban, and we tore off into the night like fugitives running from the gates of hell.

That night changed me.

I understood, in a way I never had before, how fragile life was. One wrong color. One wrong affiliation. One wrong home—and you could lose everything. I was caught in a war I didn't sign up for. A pawn in someone else's game.

But I wasn't powerless. I began to read the signs—spiritual, emotional, physical. Fear stopped being just a warning; it became a compass.

And I knew, though I didn't dare say it yet—

This couldn't last.

David's brother called one night from New York; voice ragged through the static. He was in trouble—someone was after him—and he needed to disappear. I thought maybe it would be good for David, something outside of his own chaos to focus on.

I was wrong.

When Marcus arrived, the energy shifted. They were brothers in blood only. David was caramel-skinned and loud; Marcus was tall, lean, and quiet, carrying a darkness that made people shrink without him saying a word. David called him "the devil."

I didn't understand at first. Marcus was polite, even kind. He helped around the house, gave me space to breathe. But under the surface, there was something I couldn't name— something that made the hair on my arms rise without reason.

We rented a home with another of David's friends, Nokie. His addictions would reveal themselves later, but at the time he was just the man who brought us electronics for cheap— TVs, cameras, equipment that kick-started our filming business. His wife and two little girls, Bubbles and Keke, filled the space my son had left behind.

They became my shadows. Every morning, they'd burst into my room barefoot and giggling, asking to play. I braided their dolls' hair, taught them to color inside the lines, sang the old gospel lullabies my mother used to hum on her good days.

Their laughter was like tiny bells, chasing away the heaviness in my chest. For a few hours each day, I could pretend I was whole. They clung to me like I was the safest place in the world—and maybe, for a little while, I was.

We made peanut butter sandwiches in the kitchen while they drew hearts and stars on my arms with washable markers. I told them stories about angels and brave little girls who escaped the dark with only faith and fire. They believed me. And for a moment, I believed myself.

Loving them was like borrowing sunlight. For a while, we were a strange little family, bound not by blood but by survival.

One afternoon, we were curled up on the living room floor—crayons scattered, cartoons murmuring in the background. I was helping Keke trace her hand when the channel switched to a breaking news alert.

A mugshot flashed across the screen. My chest locked. I knew that face.

Nokie's son. The same young man who'd been lounging in our living room days before.

Wanted for murder.

The innocence in that house cracked instantly. The air grew still. The children kept laughing, unaware that the world outside had just slipped through the door.

That day, I understood something I hadn't wanted to face— darkness could sit right beside you. Quiet. Smiling. Deadly.

Survival always came at a cost.

And I was starting to understand the currency.

Chapter 15: A Ransom on My Name

It was supposed to be a getaway—a breath I desperately needed. David was in jail. I was in California with Matthew, living in that strange space between escape and clarity, trying to make sense of the life I had built around danger.

The sun felt warmer there. My laughter came easier. For a fleeting moment, I let myself believe I could still reclaim peace.

Then Matthew got a call.

I knew it was bad before he spoke—the way his face dropped, like a curtain falling. He said Nokie—one of David's people—was claiming I'd been kidnapped. That I was being held for ransom. That Matthew needed to pay if he ever wanted to see me again.

I laughed at first. It sounded like the plot of a bad movie. Too outrageous to believe. But the laughter died quickly. It wasn't a joke. This was the world I had married into—where lies could become weapons, and your name could be used as currency.

When we returned to Nashville, the situation escalated. I found myself in the back of a car with Matthew and two undercover officers, listening to them plan a sting operation in a grocery store parking lot. They spoke like I wasn't even there—like I was a case file instead of a person.

They went through with it. Cash was dropped. They waited for a kidnapper who didn't exist.

When someone finally did show up—days, maybe weeks later—he was arrested. I watched from the sidelines as his life fell apart, knowing his wife and two little girls were living in the same house where I laid my head at night. I heard them crying in the dark. I listened to her ask questions I couldn't answer. And in that silence, I realized how far the chaos had spread—how it had seeped into places and people I never meant to harm.

That day, something in me cracked. Trust began to rot at the root. I started to see the truth: this wasn't protection. It was possession dressed as loyalty. Control disguised as love.

And I knew I needed a way out.

When David came home from jail, he was even harder than before—silent, closed-off, the edges of him sharper. I didn't push for details. I just watched the weight settle in his eyes.

That's when I booked two flights to Orlando without telling him. Maybe, I thought, his mother could soften what prison had hardened.

When I handed him the ticket, he looked at it like it was written in a language he didn't understand.

"What's this?" he asked.

"A break," I said. "A reset."

He didn't smile. But he didn't say no.

In Orlando, his mother met us in the hotel lobby where she worked. Small, round, glowing like only an Aquarius could. She hugged me before she hugged him. "So you're the one," she said. And in that moment, I felt seen—not as the girl who'd been running, surviving, fighting—but as someone worthy of love. She called me her daughter. And for the first time in a long time, I believed it.

Her home was modest, a short drive from her job. Each morning, she brewed strong coffee and played R&B that drifted through the screen doors, wrapping the apartment in peace I hadn't felt in years.

For a few days, we lived like a family. She cooked meals from scratch—cakes, pies, meatloaf so rich it felt like a celebration. She insisted I eat enough for two, even though I wasn't pregnant. Around her kitchen table, with its mismatched chairs and easy laughter, it was almost possible to forget the world had ever fallen apart.

David softened. Just a little. He joked with his sister. He smiled without suspicion. And for a while, I saw the man I first met—the one who made promises in the dark and danced with daylight dreams.

One evening, we wandered through Universal Studios, riding everything, the lights reflecting on the water like stars that had fallen close enough to touch. David squeezed my hand.

"Maybe this is what peace feels like," he said.

I nodded. But inside, I knew—peace wasn't a place you arrived at. It was a decision. A surrender.

And we weren't there yet.

Chapter 16: The Door That Wouldn't Close

We flew back from Orlando in silence.

David didn't say much, but I could feel the shift in him—the way his shoulders tensed, the subtle distance in his gaze. He hadn't outright said whether he believed my story about the ransom. But something in his body language made me wonder. Still, he agreed to return to the house. Maybe he thought facing it would clear the fog. Or maybe... he was just tired of running.

The plane touched down, but my spirit didn't. There was a weight in my chest, a quiet dread that whispered we were stepping back into something we weren't ready for.

As we pulled up to the house, something felt wrong. Tangibly wrong. The kind of wrong that makes the air taste different. Even before we reached the door, my instincts screamed.

Still, I opened it.

And there they were.

Nokie. David's brother. Strangers I'd never seen before. All of them gathered in the living room, armed like they were waiting for a war to begin. The tension was alive in the walls, vibrating through the floor. I didn't speak. Just pushed past them, heart hammering, and darted down to the basement where my bedroom was.

Then it happened.

A shuffle.

A scream.

A gunshot.

And then—silence.

The sound sliced through me like the last beat of a dying drum. I froze, breath caught in my throat. Then came the footsteps—quick, heavy, and coming fast.

I didn't wait.

I flew up the stairs barefoot, bursting through the front door into the night. I ran, lungs burning, legs barely touching the ground, until I reached the first house with a light on. I pounded on the door, desperate, pleading.

A man opened it—Mexican, maybe mid-30s. His eyes widened when he saw the fear written across my face.

"They're coming," I gasped. "Please. I just need to hide."

Without a word, he stepped aside.

I collapsed onto his couch, shaking. We sat in silence, listening to sirens scream past like angry spirits ripping through the night.

Later, David called. His voice was torn, panicked.

"They kidnapped me," he said.

The house had been torn apart. Our belongings stolen. Our peace—what little was left—obliterated.

This wasn't a robbery.

It was a message.

One I'd never forget.

I left that home behind and rented a small condo on Bell Road. Alone.

For a while, things calmed. Nokie was eventually arrested. And that summer, we flew back to New Orleans. Hope was thin, fragile as glass, but I clutched it anyway. His father was there this time—and he wasn't gentle.

He wouldn't let me near the house. Wouldn't let me see my son.

I was crushed—but not defeated. I didn't want to fight. I wanted to be smart, respectful. So I tried something else.

I walked into a downtown casino—the only place with a nearby Western Union. My plan was simple: send him money. A gesture. A signal that I meant no harm, that I only wanted to be part of my son's life.

But fate had other plans.

As soon as I handed over my ID, the woman behind the counter hesitated. Her eyes narrowed.

"You're underage," she said. And just like that—security was called.

Before I knew it, David and I were being led to a back room. Interrogated like criminals beneath the glittering lights of a casino that smelled like stale dreams and cigarette ash.

I called my son's father—begged him to help, to explain the truth.

He didn't.

Worse—he lied. Said David had threatened him.

That lie hung in the air thicker than the smoke around us. My heart dropped. I couldn't breathe. All I'd ever wanted was to see my son—and now I was drowning in accusations, locked doors, and quiet betrayals.

Eventually, they let us go.

We boarded the first flight out of New Orleans—exhausted, hearts heavy, carrying nothing but grief, silence, and the kind of pain only a mother understands.

Back in Tennessee, David took me to one of his doctor's appointments.

That's where I saw it.

The truth.

The nurse pulled me aside. Her eyes were kind—too kind to lie. She handed me a folder, thick with medical records. Diagnoses, treatment notes, and words I didn't fully understand but had always felt in my bones. She looked at me gently and said:

"If he didn't disclose this before marriage, you can annul it."

I sat there, numb. Every nerve in my body buzzed with panic. A thousand exits screamed in my head. But before I could choose one—

A pregnancy test.

Positive.

Just when I thought I had nothing left to break, life found a way to tether me again—in the most delicate, terrifying way.

A child.

Growing inside me.

I should've left.

But I stayed.

And the violence returned—sharper, colder, and this time, I had even more to lose.

Chapter 17: The Room That Held Me

There's a part of me that still goes quiet when I try to remember it all.

As if Bell Road has been swallowed by static—flickers of memory instead of full scenes.

Just flashes.

But the pieces I do remember...

I'll never forget.

We argued.

I don't even know how it started—maybe it didn't matter. What mattered was how quickly it turned. Something in him shifted, like a mask falling off. The air grew sharp, suffocating. He blocked the door. Took my phone. And just like that, I was trapped.

Three days.

Three days in that room.

No sunlight.

No food.

No way out.

Only his voice—louder than my thoughts—and the sound of my own breath folding into silent prayers.

He hit me.

First with his hands. Then... with a mallet.

My legs bloomed in bruises—dark, unnatural. Like spilled ink across a page I never meant to write. I stopped sleeping. Stopped eating. Kindness became a foreign language. I could feel myself fading—slowly disappearing from my own body, as if I were watching someone else's nightmare from behind fogged glass.

Eventually, he collapsed—his rage finally burning itself out. While he slept, I moved like a shadow. Quiet. Shaking. Barely human.

I found his phone.

No plan. No words.

I called one of his cousins and whispered the only thing I could:

"Come get me."

They did.

Next stop: the police station.

I filed the report, my hands trembling so badly I could hardly hold the pen. For a moment, I believed I was free.

Safe.

Done.

But trauma doesn't follow straight lines.

It loops. It hunts. It comes back dressed in apologies.

A few hours later—there he was again.

Smooth.

Smiling.

Like nothing had ever happened.

He promised me everything.

Peace. Change. A future.

And I went back.

Not because I didn't know better.

But because something inside me still believed I could fix him.

Because I thought maybe I was broken too.

Because I didn't know where else to go.

But now—now I know.

That wasn't love.

That was survival wearing fear as a disguise.

Chapter 18: The Belly, the Stage, the Burden

By this time, I was heavily pregnant, and David wouldn't let me out of his sight—not even for a breath. He watched me constantly, as though the world might steal me away if he looked away for too long. So I moved through the city under his shadow, carrying a life inside me while pressure mounted all around. It didn't matter where we were—clubs, recording studios, smoky venues with sticky floors and blaring lights—I dragged my swollen belly through them all. Sometimes in heels, often in pain, and always in silence.

David was the face everyone saw. The voice. The presence. He lit up rooms with that untouchable mix of charm and bravado that made people stop and pay attention. But behind that glow, I was the one grinding gears. I booked the shows, managed the artists, handled the logistics nobody else could or would. I wrote bios, built websites, designed logos, opened royalty accounts, negotiated contracts, and juggled overlapping dreams. I didn't just support him—I sustained the entire operation. I was the mother of his child, yes, but I was also the mother of his career.

Together, we built an album—a full body of work stitched together with the thread of our chaos. It was born in violence, passion, desperation, and the flickering hope that maybe music could save us. Somehow, it caught the attention of people who mattered. Real label heads. Real scouts. Real interest. I poured everything I had into making it happen, down to my last ounce of energy. And when they came to Nashville to see what the city had to offer, they didn't just see David. They saw *us*. They saw *me*.

But no matter how far we climbed, David always found a way to spiral. A suspended license. A missed court date. Another accusation. And every time, I was the one untangling the mess—calling lawyers, pulling favors, scraping together bail money like it was part of my job description. Because that's what I believed a wife was supposed to do. I thought if I could just keep him in motion—keep him busy, focused, performing—I could keep us safe.

But the truth was harsher than that. I wasn't managing a man or a career. I was managing a storm. A dangerous, unraveling force I couldn't stop or slow down. And I wasn't just carrying a child—I was carrying the crushing weight of being everyone's everything. My body was breaking down. My spirit, even more so. But still, I kept going. Because when you're in survival mode, stopping isn't an option—it's a luxury you can't afford.

Chapter 19: Birth and the Breaking Point

I gave birth to my son—David Jr.—on a cold December day in 2010, inside Baptist Hospital in Nashville. The irony was sharp and bitter: this was a birth we had planned to the minute, and yet David nearly missed it entirely. He dropped me off at the hospital with a kiss on the cheek and a promise to be right back, then disappeared into the city like smoke vanishing in winter air. Hours passed. My contractions came steady, crashing over me like waves, and still, he didn't return. Instead, one of the other artist's girlfriends arrived to sit beside me. Her eyes were quiet, her mouth shut tight about where he might be.

Just as I was beginning to push, he finally burst through the door. His eyes were wide, electric with chaos, his energy too loud, too wild for a delivery room. There was no time to speak, no time to ask where he'd been. I gritted my teeth, bore down, and brought life into the world.

A perfect, healthy, 7-pound baby boy.

The moment they placed him on my chest, something inside me softened. A kind of peace I didn't think I was capable of washed over me. I had carried this child through so much— through late nights filled with music and shouting, through motel rooms and broken promises, through a love that often didn't feel like love at all. And now, here he was. Whole. Real. Mine.

But the peace didn't last. As I looked up, I realized the room had fallen silent—not in awe, but in something colder. The nurses looked away. David stood frozen. My son's skin was light, too light, in stark contrast to David's deep brown complexion. I didn't flinch. I didn't question. To me, this was our child. I had no doubt. Because it wasn't biology that had carried us through—it was loyalty, survival, and love. And love, I believed, wasn't defined by skin tone.

David couldn't see past it.

The moment the baby was born, something in him shifted— disconnected. He turned his back and walked out of the room. And just like that, what little stability we had unraveled.

At first, it was subtle. He became distant, colder. His voice lost its warmth, his touch its softness. There were fewer calls, shorter visits. Then came the arguments—sharp, unrelenting. Questions loaded like weapons. Accusations spoken in riddles and rage. I came home from the hospital with a newborn in my arms and a partner who no longer looked at me with love, but with suspicion.

He didn't leave me outright—he just stopped coming home. Nights blurred into days, days into weeks. Rumors reached me before he did. He was staying with friends, crashing on couches, circling close but never present. And when he did return, it was like weather—loud, sudden, angry. He came in like a storm, stirred everything up, and vanished when it calmed.

Then one day, I walked into chaos. My home had been vandalized again. My car was gone. When I confronted him, he barely blinked before pointing the finger at Chris—a friend of mine he had never liked. He claimed Chris was the father of my child. His voice cracked with venom, but I saw through it. He didn't believe it out of truth—he believed it out of fear and pride.

And deep down, I knew... he had done this. Not just to my things, but to us.

Chapter 20: Unraveling at the Seams

I thought maybe things would shift—that the distance had cooled the chaos that somehow we could begin again. So I moved. I rented a new townhouse in Davidlin, Tennessee. It was clean, quiet, and carried the kind of stillness I had been craving. David stayed behind in Nashville, and for a time, we lived apart. I needed the space—to breathe, to think, to stitch myself back together while caring for a newborn. I was healing, slowly, silently.

But trouble has a way of finding you, especially when it wears a familiar face.

It was a rainy afternoon when David came to pick up our son, little David Jr. He was only supposed to take him for a visit, bring him back safely. That was all. But the rain made the roads slick and unforgiving. He hydroplaned, wrecking the car. And instead of stopping, instead of calling for help like any father should, he drove the vehicle all the way back to Davidlin on a rim—sparks flying from the pavement like desperate fireworks. I heard the metal scream against the street before I even saw him.

Then came the lights.

The sirens.

The guns.

Police swarmed the house as if war had arrived at our doorstep. David collapsed across the back seat, baby David beside him, quiet and wide-eyed. I ran outside, heart in my throat, and pulled my baby from the wreckage, clutching him to my chest like a shield. All I could think was: Get him to safety. But then I heard David's voice—shouting, struggling, full of rage—and when I turned, I saw the officers beating him. They slammed his head into the side of the cruiser like he wasn't human.

I screamed.

"Stop! That's my husband!"

But they didn't stop. They didn't hear me—or worse, they didn't care. They mocked me. Laughed at me. Treated me like I was invisible. And when I tried to get closer to him, to help him, to make them see he was a person, they maced me instead.

The fire in my eyes felt biblical. My skin burned. My spirit shattered. And somehow, the chemicals touched my baby too. I held him as we both cried—his tiny body pressed against mine, both of us choking on pain, wheeled into the hospital like casualties of someone else's war. And then the nurse came in, her eyes wide, her mouth tight with something heavy. I'll never forget what she said next:

"You're pregnant."

Pregnant? Again?

I had just given life. My body wasn't ready. My heart definitely wasn't. So I said nothing. Not to the nurse. Not to David. Not even to myself. I buried it deep beneath the rubble of everything else I was trying to survive.

Weeks passed. Then months. David remained locked up in the Davidlin jail, and the silence that filled our home grew thick—like grief, like fog, like punishment. I was no longer welcome there. Kicked out of Davidlin like a criminal, exiled from a town that didn't know how to hold my story. I moved into a weekly motel, carrying what little I had: two babies, a suitcase of worn-out clothes, and a soul unraveling at the seams.

Each night was a quiet prayer beneath the dim flicker of a motel lamp. Each bottle I warmed, each diaper I changed, every tear I wiped—from theirs or mine—was a quiet declaration: I'm still here. I'm still standing.

Eventually, with nowhere else to turn, I called Matthew.

I didn't know what I was expecting—judgment, resentment, maybe even a dial tone. But he answered like he always had—calm, steady, offering a kind of silence that let me breathe. Somewhere between the words I said and the ones I couldn't, I think he understood. He had always known more than I admitted. David had started questioning the paternity of our son—pointing out how light-skinned he was, how different. And now, I was pregnant again.

Matthew saw my son and didn't need a test. He knew. But he never pressed. Never claimed. He simply listened, letting me give him the version of the truth I could live with. And still, he stayed.

I told him I might terminate the pregnancy. That I didn't feel ready. That I didn't know how to carry another life when mine felt so shattered. And yet, somewhere in me, something whispered: Don't.

Because even after everything, David was still my husband. And no matter how far from love we had drifted—no matter how many times that love hurt—some small piece of me still felt bound to him. By our vows. By our children. By a hope that flickered like a dying candle, but hadn't quite gone out.

Eventually, I left that motel behind and moved to Brentwood. A new city. A new roof. A new version of hope. But I learned something in that move—the past doesn't surrender just because you change addresses. It follows. Sometimes quietly. Sometimes with sirens.

But always.

Chapter 16: The Door That Wouldn't Close

We flew back from Orlando in silence.

David didn't say much, but I could feel the shift in him—the way his shoulders tensed, the subtle distance in his gaze. He hadn't outright said whether he believed my story about the ransom. But something in his body language made me wonder. Still, he agreed to return to the house. Maybe he thought facing it would clear the fog. Or maybe... he was just tired of running.

The plane touched down, but my spirit didn't. There was a weight in my chest, a quiet dread that whispered we were stepping back into something we weren't ready for.

As we pulled up to the house, something felt wrong. Tangibly wrong. The kind of wrong that makes the air taste different. Even before we reached the door, my instincts screamed.

Still, I opened it.

And there they were.

Nathan. David's brother. Strangers I'd never seen before. All of them gathered in the living room, armed like they were waiting for a war to begin. The tension was alive in the walls, vibrating through the floor. I didn't speak. Just pushed past them, heart hammering, and darted down to the basement where my bedroom was.

Then it happened.

A shuffle.

A scream.

A gunshot.

And then—silence.

The sound sliced through me like the last beat of a dying drum. I froze, breath caught in my throat. Then came the footsteps—quick, heavy, and coming fast.

I didn't wait.

I flew up the stairs barefoot, bursting through the front door into the night. I ran, lungs burning, legs barely touching the ground, until I reached the first house with a light on. I pounded on the door, desperate, pleading.

A man opened it—Mexican, maybe mid-30s. His eyes widened when he saw the fear written across my face.

"They're coming," I gasped. "Please. I just need to hide."

Without a word, he stepped aside.

I collapsed onto his couch, shaking. We sat in silence, listening to sirens scream past like angry spirits ripping through the night.

Later, David called. His voice was torn, panicked.

"They kidnapped me," he said.

The house had been torn apart. Our belongings stolen. Our peace—what little was left—obliterated.

This wasn't a robbery.

It was a message.

One I'd never forget.

I left that home behind and rented a small condo on Bell Road. Alone.

For a while, things calmed. Nathan was eventually arrested. And that summer, we flew back to New Orleans. Hope was thin, fragile as glass, but I clutched it anyway. His father was there this time—and he wasn't gentle.

He wouldn't let me near the house. Wouldn't let me see my son.

I was crushed—but not defeated. I didn't want to fight. I wanted to be smart, respectful. So I tried something else.

I walked into a downtown casino—the only place with a nearby Western Union. My plan was simple: send him money. A gesture. A signal that I meant no harm, that I only wanted to be part of my son's life.

But fate had other plans.

As soon as I handed over my ID, the woman behind the counter hesitated. Her eyes narrowed.

"You're underage," she said. And just like that—security was called.

Before I knew it, David and I were being led to a back room. Interrogated like criminals beneath the glittering lights of a casino that smelled like stale dreams and cigarette ash.

I called my son's father—begged him to help, to explain the truth.

He didn't.

Worse—he lied. Said David had threatened him.

That lie hung in the air thicker than the smoke around us. My heart dropped. I couldn't breathe. All I'd ever wanted was to see my son—and now I was drowning in accusations, locked doors, and quiet betrayals.

Eventually, they let us go.

We boarded the first flight out of New Orleans—exhausted, hearts heavy, carrying nothing but grief, silence, and the kind of pain only a mother understands.

Back in Tennessee, David took me to one of his doctor's appointments.

That's where I saw it.

The truth.

The nurse pulled me aside. Her eyes were kind—too kind to lie. She handed me a folder, thick with medical records. Diagnoses, treatment notes, and words I didn't fully understand but had always felt in my bones. She looked at me gently and said:

"If he didn't disclose this before marriage, you can annul it."

I sat there, numb. Every nerve in my body buzzed with panic. A thousand exits screamed in my head. But before I could choose one—

A pregnancy test.

Positive.

Just when I thought I had nothing left to break, life found a way to tether me again—in the most delicate, terrifying way.

A child.

Growing inside me.

I should've left.

But I stayed.

And the violence returned—sharper, colder, and this time, I had even more to lose.

Chapter 17: The Room That Held Me

There's a part of me that still goes quiet when I try to remember it all.

As if Bell Road has been swallowed by static— flickers of memory instead of full scenes.

Just flashes.

But the pieces I do remember...

I'll never forget.

We argued.

I don't even know how it started—maybe it didn't matter. What mattered was how quickly it turned. Something in him shifted, like a mask falling off. The air grew sharp, suffocating. He blocked the door. Took my phone. And just like that, I was trapped.

Three days.

Three days in that room.

No sunlight.

No food.

No way out.

Only his voice—louder than my thoughts—and the sound of my own breath folding into silent prayers.

He hit me.

First with his hands. Then... with a mallet.

My legs bloomed in bruises—dark, unnatural. Like spilled ink across a page I never meant to write. I stopped sleeping. Stopped eating. Kindness became a foreign language. I could feel myself fading—slowly disappearing from my own body, as if I were watching someone else's nightmare from behind fogged glass.

Eventually, he collapsed—his rage finally burning itself out. While he slept, I moved like a shadow. Quiet. Shaking. Barely human.

I found his phone.

No plan. No words.

I called one of his cousins and whispered the only thing I could:

"Come get me."

They did.

Next stop: the police station.

I filed the report, my hands trembling so badly I could hardly hold the pen. For a moment, I believed I was free.

Safe.

Done.

But trauma doesn't follow straight lines.

It loops. It hunts. It comes back dressed in apologies.

A few hours later—there he was again.

Smooth.

Smiling.

Like nothing had ever happened.

He promised me everything.

Peace. Change. A future.

And I went back.

Not because I didn't know better.

But because something inside me still believed I could fix him.

Because I thought maybe I was broken too.

Because I didn't know where else to go.

But now—now I know.

That wasn't love.

That was survival wearing fear as a disguise.

Chapter 18: The Belly, the Stage, the Burden

By this time, I was heavily pregnant, and David wouldn't let me out of his sight—not even for a breath. He watched me constantly, as though the world might steal me away if he looked away for too long. So I moved through the city under his shadow, carrying a life inside me while pressure mounted all around. It didn't matter where we were—clubs, recording studios, smoky venues with sticky floors and blaring lights—I dragged my swollen belly through them all. Sometimes in heels, often in pain, and always in silence.

David was the face everyone saw. The voice. The presence. He lit up rooms with that untouchable mix of charm and bravado that made people stop and pay attention. But behind that glow, I was the one grinding gears. I booked the shows, managed the artists, handled the logistics nobody else could or would. I wrote bios, built websites, designed logos, opened royalty accounts, negotiated contracts, and juggled overlapping dreams. I didn't just support him—I sustained the entire operation. I was the mother of his child, yes, but I was also the mother of his career.

Together, we built an album—a full body of work stitched together with the thread of our chaos. It was born in violence, passion, desperation, and the flickering hope that maybe music could save us. Somehow, it caught the attention of people who mattered. Real label heads. Real scouts. Real interest. I poured everything I had into making it happen, down to my last ounce of energy. And when they came to Nashville to see what the city had to offer, they didn't just see David. They saw *us*. They saw *me*.

But no matter how far we climbed, David always found a way to spiral. A suspended license. A missed court date. Another accusation. And every time, I was the one untangling the mess—calling lawyers, pulling favors, scraping together bail money like it was part of my job description. Because that's what I believed a wife was supposed to do. I thought if I could just keep him in motion—keep him busy, focused, performing—I could keep us safe.

But the truth was harsher than that. I wasn't managing a man or a career. I was managing a storm. A dangerous, unraveling force I couldn't stop or slow down. And I wasn't just carrying a child—I was carrying the crushing weight of being everyone's everything. My body was breaking down.

My spirit, even more so. But still, I kept going. Because when you're in survival mode, stopping isn't an option—it's a luxury you can't afford.

Chapter 19: Birth and the Breaking Point

I gave birth to my son—David Jr.—on a cold December day in 2010, inside Baptist Hospital in Nashville. The irony was sharp and bitter: this was a birth we had planned to the minute, and yet David nearly missed it entirely. He dropped me off at the hospital with a kiss on the cheek and a promise to be right back, then disappeared into the city like smoke vanishing in winter air. Hours passed. My contractions came steady, crashing over me like waves, and still, he didn't return. Instead, one of the other artist's girlfriends arrived to sit beside me. Her eyes were quiet, her mouth shut tight about where he might be.

Just as I was beginning to push, he finally burst through the door. His eyes were wide, electric with chaos, his energy too loud, too wild for a delivery room. There was no time to speak, no time to ask where he'd been. I gritted my teeth, bore down, and brought life into the world.

A perfect, healthy, 7-pound baby boy.

The moment they placed him on my chest, something inside me softened. A kind of peace I didn't think I was capable of washed over me. I had carried this child through so much— through late nights filled with music and shouting, through motel rooms and broken promises, through a love that often didn't feel like love at all. And now, here he was. Whole. Real. Mine.

But the peace didn't last. As I looked up, I realized the room had fallen silent—not in awe, but in something colder. The nurses looked away. David stood frozen. My son's skin was light, too light, in stark contrast to David's deep brown complexion. I didn't flinch. I didn't question. To me, this was our child. I had no doubt. Because it wasn't biology that had carried us through—it was loyalty, survival, and love. And love, I believed, wasn't defined by skin tone.

David couldn't see past it.

The moment the baby was born, something in him shifted—disconnected. He turned his back and walked out of the room. And just like that, what little stability we had unraveled.

At first, it was subtle. He became distant, colder. His voice lost its warmth, his touch its softness. There were fewer calls, shorter visits. Then came the arguments—sharp, unrelenting. Questions loaded like weapons. Accusations spoken in riddles and rage. I came home from the hospital with a newborn in my arms and a partner who no longer looked at me with love, but with suspicion.

He didn't leave me outright—he just stopped coming home. Nights blurred into days, days into weeks. Rumors reached me before he did. He was staying with friends, crashing on couches, circling close but never present. And when he did return, it was like weather—loud, sudden, angry. He came in like a storm, stirred everything up, and vanished when it calmed.

Then one day, I walked into chaos. My home had been vandalized again. My car was gone. When I confronted him, he barely blinked before pointing the finger at Thomas—a friend of mine he had never liked. He claimed Thomas was the father of my child. His voice cracked with venom, but I saw through it. He didn't believe it out of truth—he believed it out of fear and pride.

And deep down, I knew... he had done this. Not just to my things, but to us.

Chapter 20: Unraveling at the Seams

I thought maybe things would shift—that the distance had cooled the chaos that somehow we could begin again. So I moved. I rented a new townhouse in Franklin, Tennessee. It was clean, quiet, and carried the kind of stillness I had been craving. David stayed behind in Nashville, and for a time, we lived apart. I needed the space—to breathe, to think, to stitch myself back together while caring for a newborn. I was healing, slowly, silently.

But trouble has a way of finding you, especially when it wears a familiar face.

It was a rainy afternoon when David came to pick up our son, little David Jr. He was only supposed to take him for a visit, bring him back safely. That was all. But the rain made the roads slick and unforgiving. He hydroplaned, wrecking the car. And instead of stopping, instead of calling for help like any father should, he drove the vehicle all the way back to Franklin on a rim—sparks flying from the pavement like desperate fireworks. I heard the metal scream against the street before I even saw him.

Then came the lights.

The sirens.

The guns.

Police swarmed the house as if war had arrived at our doorstep. David collapsed across the back seat, baby David beside him, quiet and wide-eyed. I ran outside, heart in my throat, and pulled my baby from the wreckage, clutching him to my chest like a shield. All I could think was: Get him to safety. But then I heard David's voice—shouting, struggling, full of rage—and when I turned, I saw the officers beating him. They slammed his head into the side of the cruiser like he wasn't human.

I screamed.

"Stop! That's my husband!"

But they didn't stop. They didn't hear me—or worse, they didn't care. They mocked me. Laughed at me. Treated me like I was invisible. And when I tried to get closer to him, to help him, to make them see he was a person, they maced me instead.

The fire in my eyes felt biblical. My skin burned. My spirit shattered. And somehow, the chemicals touched my baby too. I held him as we both cried—his tiny body pressed against mine, both of us choking on pain, wheeled into the hospital like casualties of someone else's war. And then the nurse came in, her eyes wide, her mouth tight with something heavy. I'll never forget what she said next:

"You're pregnant."

Pregnant? Again?

I had just given life. My body wasn't ready. My heart definitely wasn't. So I said nothing. Not to the nurse. Not to David. Not even to myself. I buried it deep beneath the rubble of everything else I was trying to survive.

Weeks passed. Then months. David remained locked up in the Franklin jail, and the silence that filled our home grew thick—like grief, like fog, like punishment. I was no longer welcome there. Kicked out of Franklin like a criminal, exiled from a town that didn't know how to hold my story. I moved into a weekly motel, carrying what little I had: two babies, a suitcase of worn-out clothes, and a soul unraveling at the seams.

Each night was a quiet prayer beneath the dim flicker of a motel lamp. Each bottle I warmed, each diaper I changed, every tear I wiped—from theirs or mine—was a quiet declaration: I'm still here. I'm still standing.

One night David showed up to the hotel in a rage, demanding to know who the father of my child was. In the middle of the argument, I got up from the bed and he shoved me into the wall. When I came to, I was sitting in the bathtub, the shower running, my clothes soaked through, and David was jumping up and down, yelling at me to stop playing. I stared at him blankly, unable to recognize him. I looked at my body in the tub and couldn't understand how I got there. Panic gripped me as I screamed, "What did you do to me?" My mind was blank—I couldn't remember my name, my age, or even where I was. It wasn't until I heard my son's cries that reality snapped back. I leapt from the tub, ran past David, and curled myself around my baby, praying to God for strength. David, stunned, left us there.

Eventually, with nowhere else to turn, I called Matthew.

I didn't know what I was expecting—judgment, resentment, maybe even a dial tone. But he answered like he always had—calm, steady, offering a kind of silence that let me breathe. Somewhere between the words I said and the ones I couldn't, I think he understood. He had always known more than I admitted. David had started questioning the paternity of our son—pointing out how light-skinned he was, how different. And now, I was pregnant again.

Matthew saw my son and didn't need a test. He knew. But he never pressed. Never claimed. He simply listened, letting me give him the version of the truth I could live with. And still, he stayed.

I told him I might terminate the pregnancy. That I didn't feel ready. That I didn't know how to carry another life when mine felt so shattered. And yet, somewhere in me, something whispered: Don't.

Because even after everything, David was still my husband. And no matter how far from love we had drifted—no matter how many times that love hurt—some small piece of me still felt bound to him. By our vows. By our children. By a hope that flickered like a dying candle, but hadn't quite gone out.

Eventually, I left that motel behind and moved to Brentwood. A new city. A new roof. A new version of hope. But I learned something in that move—the past doesn't surrender just because you change addresses. It follows. Sometimes quietly. Sometimes with sirens.

But always.

Chapter 21: The Airport Collapse

God, Are You Listening?

Before Dawn was even a whisper in the world, my body tried to tell me something my mind had been too busy to hear.

I was in Miami again with Matthew—another brief escape from the weight of home. But something felt off. I ignored the signals. The heaviness in my chest. The light-headed moments. I told myself I was just tired, just overwhelmed. But the truth was, my body was screaming while I kept pretending it could still carry everything.

Then, at the gate before takeoff, I collapsed.

One moment I was upright, the next I was drifting. Faces blurred. Lights dimmed. Voices faded into a language I couldn't understand. When I woke up, I was strapped to a hospital bed in Hialeah—barely able to move, surrounded by signs I couldn't read, with strangers peering down at me like I was a ghost come back to life.

Everything was written in Spanish. The staff moved quickly but spoke softly, urgently. One doctor walked in and said "blockage" and "surgery" and that was it. No one explained anything more. No one told me where I really was. It felt like

I had slipped into another world—one where no one could hear me, and I didn't even know how to cry for help.

David was still locked up, unreachable. But his brother from New York was in Nashville with David, jr at the time. Without hesitation, he flew into Miami and rescued me— like an angel dispatched from a broken heaven.

We flew together to Orlando, where his family was gathering for his sister's Sweet 16. I tried to show up for her, to be present, to pretend I was okay. But my body betrayed me again. I collapsed a second time.

This time, they rushed me into the hospital and didn't let me leave. The pain was sharp, my breath shallow. My mom flew in with the kind of storm that only she could bring—part worry, part judgment, all control.

I underwent surgery. A stent. A temporary fix to a body that had been burning the candle at both ends for far too long. That's when they said it again.

"You're pregnant and It's a girl"

Another life growing inside me while I was barely holding onto my own. Another miracle wrapped in crisis. Another moment where God whispered, *You're still here.* And now I was now forced to stay on bed rest.

Dawn came into this world in Smyrna, Tennessee—at the big hospital just off the freeway, 13 months after her brother. And just as light skinned. She was a perfect 8 pounds, but the moment she emerged, the room turned cold with panic. Her tiny body was completely blue, still, like the breath of God hadn't reached her yet. The umbilical cord had wrapped itself around her neck twice, binding her before she had a chance to speak her name into the world. But as soon as it loosened, she stirred. She wiggled. She lived.

She looked nothing like I expected—more like a porcelain doll than a newborn. Delicate. Radiant. Divine. I was stunned, as if beauty itself had whispered into the room and laid gently in my arms.

David was there briefly. Freshly released. His mother had flown in from Florida, worried after the last hospital scare. She stayed for a week, helping where she could. Matthew stopped by and left flowers but forgot to sign the card indicating who it was from, so David got upset and left. Then my own mother arrived, just in time for my discharge. I should've felt joy. Gratitude. Relief. But as I left the hospital, something was wrong.

I was so weak I could barely stand. My body didn't feel like my own. I laid down, hoping it was just exhaustion—but it wasn't sleep that wrapped around me. It felt like the veil between this world and the next had parted. I couldn't speak. I couldn't move. My soul felt like it was slipping. Dying.

It took everything in me to rise from that bed, and when I finally opened the door, I collapsed. My mother heard the thud and found me there, unresponsive. She screamed for help. The ambulance came fast, and so did the diagnosis—a blood clot. A silent killer that could've taken me from my babies.

They told me later that she saved my life.

From that day forward, I was on blood thinners, two-week doctor visits, and the daily battle of caring for two small children while trying to heal a body—and a soul—that had been through too much. I had survived again, but I was exhausted. I was alive, but I didn't feel whole. Not yet.

Then came the argument that changed everything. The moment I realized that David was not my kids' father, it was Matthew.

It was one of those nights—the kind where the tension in the air felt like lightning about to strike. He kicked in the door to our townhouse, not with fear or urgency, but rage. I can still hear the splintering wood. Still feel the chill of the garage door slamming behind me. He locked me in there, like I was something to be contained, while our one-year-old son and newborn daughter lay sleeping inside.

I pounded the walls, cried out to God—*Is this what love has become?*

The neighbors must have heard because the police came. But by then, the damage had already been done. A month later, I was evicted. Just like that—no cushion, no warning, no mercy for a new mother with two babies, one barely out of the womb.

We drifted again, this time into the Hilton. A nice hotel on the outside, but when you're holding two children and your heart feels like a cracked mirror, even luxury can feel cold.

We stayed there about a month—long enough for the staff to know us, long enough for the walls to feel temporary.

Desperate for a sense of permanence, I tried to buy a house in Brentwood. I wanted something solid, something mine. I flew my mother in, hoping she'd co-sign for me. But as soon as she stepped into the house, she wrinkled her nose. Said she didn't like it. And just like that, her help vanished. I stood there in silence as she left, holding the weight of her refusal in my chest like a cinder block. Again, I was on my own.

My rental history was a mess, a trail of storms and displacement, but then I met Mark. He didn't judge me when I told him everything. He just listened, nodded, and offered help. He agreed to co-sign an apartment with me—and not out of pity, but from a place of real grace. His sister and I hit it off instantly. She saw me, really saw me, and welcomed me like family. They even invited me to a family gathering in Memphis. And for a moment, in the middle of all that laughter, food, and familiar chaos—I felt like I was part of something whole. Something healing.

After Marcus helped open a door, Matthew kept trying to hold it open. When I told him I was overwhelmed—juggling babies, doctor's appointments, and recovery—he introduced me to Cleopatra. She was calm, warm, dependable in a way that made you want to breathe again. She eventually moved into the same apartment complex as mine, and almost instantly, we were like sisters. Then came Jazmin, her friend from Virginia. Another soul who didn't hesitate to help. Together, they offered me something I hadn't had in years: a break.

When Dawn was still small and my body needed healing, they took her back to Virginia for a week so I could rest and undergo my treatments without the constant fear of collapsing with a baby in my arms. Their kindness felt divine—like God was showing me that I didn't always have to be everything for everyone.

After they returned, I took the children to Florida to stay with David's grandmother. The tension between me and David had grown unbearable, but I still hoped for change. He was released from jail again and this time he checked himself into rehab. I gave him one final ultimatum: "Get clean, or I'm filing for divorce." For a moment, it looked like he heard me. But after barely a week, he quit. Walked out of rehab and tried to walk back into my life as if nothing had changed. After more arguments and refusals on my part, he left for

Chattanooga to stay with a cousin. I didn't chase him this time at first.

With David gone and my children safe, I tried once again to plant seeds. Cleopatra and I began planning a clothing store—something that could be ours. Something honest. We even flew to New York to explore vendors and visit my grandmother, the lights and pace of the city igniting parts of me I thought I'd lost. I wanted to build slowly, start online, make it sustainable. But Cleopatra was all-in from the start—insisting we open a storefront right away.

In the meantime, I picked up a job at Forever 21 and the kids started daycare. At first, it felt like progress. I was waking up early, dressing with purpose, clocking in like the other moms. But the math didn't add up. By the end of the month, my paycheck couldn't even cover daycare fees. I was back to zero—but this time, it stung in a new way because I was trying to do it right.

Eventually, I reached out to David again—mostly to talk about finalizing the divorce, but deep down, maybe still searching for closure. He was living in Chattanooga now, working in a small pizza shop and crashing at his cousin's place while she attended college. I loaded the kids into my new Infiniti G37 and made the drive, holding on to some fragile hope that this would be a clean, adult conversation. But peace has never lived long between us. We argued. Loud. Ugly. I packed up the kids, heart racing, and buckled them into their car seats, determined to leave.

That's when he lost it.

He flailed like a man possessed, throwing himself behind my back tires, screaming like I was about to murder him in broad daylight. His cousin came out yelling, venom in her voice, defending his chaos like a badge of loyalty. I froze, hands trembling on the wheel, unsure whether to call for help or just scream. That pause cost me. The police arrived—quick and cold. Before I could explain, I was in handcuffs, thrown into the back of a cruiser, kicking and screaming while my babies watched from the window.

They booked me in a tiny country station that smelled of mildew and judgment. I had just enough cash to bond myself out, but no ride. No one to call. They dropped me four miles from that apartment like I was trash. I walked—through hills and backroads, muscles aching, face burning, shame crawling down my spine. I kicked that door in, gathered my babies like treasure, and left.

I stayed in that apartment for a while. Long enough to hang up curtains, decorate baby rooms, long enough to hope. But peace is fragile when you've lived in survival.

Then came the spider. That thick, heavy black willow spider clinging to my wall like a shadow that refused to die. And I knew—just like the time before—peace was leaving again. Maybe it wasn't just the spider. Maybe it was the weight of everything I had tried to suppress finally crawling into the open.

After the spider incident, I knew I needed a new beginning. I found a rental home in Nashville—a place that felt less like survival and more like hope. For once, the foundation beneath my feet felt solid, and I poured that hope into my children as my divorce pushed forward.

Cleopatra left. Went back to Virginia. And opened the store... without me.

No phone call. No warning. Just my dream, repackaged in her name.

The betrayal burned deep. But I reminded myself—I didn't come this far just to give up now.

I had survived things most people wouldn't believe.

And I wasn't done yet.

I enrolled the kids in a Christian school. I thought it would be a safe place, a gentle environment where faith could meet structure, and maybe offer us all some stability.

Dawn had always had sensitive skin. I'd taken her out of diapers early because I noticed the irritation and wanted to protect her. It was something only a mother would catch— those subtle signs, the way a child squirms in discomfort. So when I dropped her off that day, I trusted they would respect that.

But they didn't.

They put a diaper on her anyway. And when I got the call from CPS to meet them at the school, I knew something was wrong. I walked into that room and saw her standing there— my baby—in a diaper that should never have touched her skin. Red marks already forming, pain written across her little body. They had taken photos. Of her. Of the rash. As if I were the danger.

And I snapped.

I wasn't just angry—I was humiliated. Violated. Heartbroken. How could they misread love so badly? How could they not see how hard I was trying?

CPS came to my home for an investigation. They turned the rooms of our lives inside out, asking questions, jotting notes. And they called David—who was now living in Florida at the time. I had actually convinced him to go. Enrolled him in school. Bought him a car. Tried to give him a path forward, even when he didn't always deserve it.

He answered their questions, and for once, even he couldn't make me look bad. Eventually, the case was dropped. But that kind of stain doesn't wash away easily. The embarrassment lingered. The shame crept into quiet moments. I felt exposed—like no matter how much I gave, how fiercely I loved, it still wasn't enough to protect my children from the world's judgment.

And yet, I kept going. Because that's what mothers do. We keep building, even when our hearts are raw. We flew to Florida and went to Disney World for the week.

Then I enrolled them into a Montessori school, craving something better for them than the chaos they had already seen too much of. And that's where the light found us again. Photographers noticed their spark—the quiet confidence, the natural charm. Soon they were signed to a talent agency, and I became the mother behind the camera: fixing collars, dabbing cheeks, cheering from behind the scenes at photo shoots, events, and commercials. The rush of it gave me purpose. We were building something new—together.

Then came a moment I didn't expect. I was at a talent show with them, just another proud mom watching from the side, when I was pulled onto the stage. Someone saw something in me—something I hadn't seen in a long time. I was selected as a model and invited to a competition in Florida. For the first time in years, someone looked at me and said I belonged somewhere special.

But just as the light rose, the shadows came clawing back.

The divorce proceedings with David had begun. And in a ruling that shattered me, the court ordered I let him keep our children for a full month. A month. Since we were married, he was their legal father no matter what. My babies—who had been my lifeline through trauma, heartbreak, and survival—were handed over, and I had to let go. I crumbled.

As part of the custody process, I was ordered to undergo a psychological evaluation. I walked in numb and walked out diagnosed: PTSD. I had never heard the words spoken over me before, not like that. I told the therapist everything—things I'd buried for years—and she explained the weight I'd been carrying wasn't weakness, it was trauma. And it had a name.

They gave me pills. Said they'd help. But all they did was numb me further—like ecstasy times five but without the euphoria. Just disconnection. I stopped taking them cold turkey and quickly learned that wasn't an option. My body revolted. I had to detox slowly, crawling my way back to some kind of normal.

At the end of that hellish month, I flew to Florida. I don't remember breathing until I had my babies in my arms. We didn't linger—I packed them up and got out of there before anything could be said or undone. But the damage had been done. The arguments didn't stop. The court battles, the power plays, the old wounds—they followed me like ghosts.

But even in that, I was learning how to fight differently. Not with fists or fire—but with vision. With love. With fierce, determined motherhood.

Around this time, Paris reentered my life—unexpectedly, but somehow right on cue, as if the universe knew I needed a reminder of who I once was. Only this time, she came with her son—my godson—and another little boy, full of wild energy and mischief. I nicknamed him Chuckie, not just for his size, but for the way he darted around like trouble with feet. Always into something.

Paris… she was frayed at the edges now. The gleam she used to carry was dulled by too much alcohol and too many losses. She drank more than I remembered, more than I was comfortable with, but I still let her in. I was working long hours, determined to rewrite the story of our lives, and I needed someone I trusted to watch my children. Who else could I ask?

But underneath it all, she was still Paris—down-to-earth, smart-mouthed, full of sass and soul. We partied. We laughed until we couldn't breathe. We cried like we used to when dreams felt real and the future hadn't yet betrayed us. For a while, it felt like we'd found each other again—not the versions life had bruised, but the girls who used to believe in escape.

By this time, I had just finished my bachelor's in business—
a degree I earned while carrying trauma, babies, and bills on
my back. And I had a vision: to open my own daycare. A
safe space. A sanctuary for children. A place that could
reflect the kind of love and structure I wished I had growing
up.

I found a broker who believed in my fire. Together, we found
a daycare for sale in Clarksville, Tennessee. I remember the
first drive like it was yesterday—me and Paris on the road,
filled with nervous excitement. We got the keys that day. I
held them in my hand like they were sacred. A symbol of
everything I had fought for.

For the next few months, life settled into a fragile rhythm.
Her son started school. She picked up my kids when I
couldn't. There were still smiles between us, still echoes of
old sisterhood. But I started to notice the cracks—how the
weight of her own demons kept pulling her under.

Then, just like that, it shattered.

We had a fallout—messy, emotional, and confusing. And
then she did the unthinkable: she took the car I had helped
her get, the very vehicle that was meant to stabilize both our

lives, and disappeared to Kansas. No warning. No goodbye. Just silence.

This would be the last time I saw her.

Two months after a sudden diagnosis, she was gone. Cancer took her body, but not her spirit. Even in the end, she was strong—stronger than I ever understood. It was like her light flared one last time before it disappeared into the stars.

I was left with a business to run, children to raise, and another wound stitched into my already torn spirit.

Taking over the daycare in Clarksville felt like stepping into my purpose. The building was old, but the vision was clear: I wanted to build a place where children could feel safe, nurtured, and loved—something I wished I had more of in my own childhood.

It was already named it the Education Station. It sat right next to a Dollar General, tucked into the heartbeat of a military town. I hired four to six teachers and created two preschool classrooms along with a drop-in care program that gave parents flexibility and peace of mind. Most of my clients were military moms, women juggling deployments and uncertainty, trying their best to raise children between the chaos.

What I didn't know at the time was that the previous owners had served in the special forces. So when a young Black woman with long dreadlocks walked in and took over, it rattled expectations. Some were skeptical, others curious— but I didn't come to prove anything. I came to serve. And soon, the walls of that daycare echoed with laughter, ABC songs, and the quiet strength of a dream unfolding.

At first, the 45-minute drive to and from Nashville every day was worth it. I poured myself into that daycare—painting walls, building lesson plans, and decorating cubbies with each child's name like they were royalty. But the strain wore on me. With two young kids and a business to run, I knew something had to change.

Then came another court hearing—yet another storm I didn't see coming.

David was there, restless, angry. Something in him snapped that day. When the judge's words didn't go his way, he tried to storm out of the courtroom. Security stepped in, but he threw them like they were paper. It all happened so fast, a blur of shouts and bodies hitting the floor.

The judge pulled me behind the bench, looked me in the eyes, and quietly handed me a one-year order of protection. I thought my divorce was finalized, but it wasn't.

"Get out of here," he said. "Now."

I didn't wait. I gathered my babies, packed up what little we had, and moved to Clarksville for good. I used every dollar I'd saved to buy my first home in cash. No landlord. No one to tell me when to leave. It was mine.

I enrolled my kids in my own daycare and ran the center full-time. For the first time, I could breathe a little. David Jr. started kindergarten. My daughter was thriving. And I— well, I felt like I was finally doing something sacred.

But then the world shifted.

When Trump was elected, the energy in Clarksville changed overnight. People stopped hiding their hatred. I was nearly run off the road multiple times—just for being Black, just for being a woman with ambition. The tension in the air was thick. Fear became a morning ritual.

Then the alarms started.

Over and over again, my daycare's security system would go off. And every time, the police came—guns drawn, like I was harboring a threat instead of teaching ABCs. I'd rush in, heart pounding, to calm everything down. But I knew—I was being targeted.

Eventually, they shut me down. Said my license couldn't be renewed. Too many children, they claimed. My building wasn't approved for the number of little lives I was serving. No grace. No warning. Just closed.

I tried running the daycare from home for a while, but it wasn't the same.

The spark was fading.

So, I made a decision that felt like surrender—but was really strength.

I sold the building. Packed up. And brought my children back to Houston.

Not because I failed.

But because I had learned how to rise. Again.

Chapter 22: A Second Chance in Houston

Returning to Houston felt like circling back to the beginning—but I was not the same woman. After everything I'd survived—the violence, the betrayals, the road trips that blurred into near madness—I was hungry for peace. My mother had rented a house for me, and for a moment, it seemed like a blessing. But old patterns don't break just because the zip code changes. She popped up unannounced, pressing opinions into spaces I was trying to rebuild.

I immediately went back to court to file a modification of the custody order for my first son. I hired a lawyer, but they kept pushing back court dates. Then, at the last minute—just a day before trial—they demanded nearly $50,000, forcing me to represent myself. My child's father only showed up once. After that, his lawyer's paralegal appeared on his behalf. In the end, they increased my child support and granted me only supervised visits in Beaumont.

For years, I had prayed just to see all three of my children together again—under one roof, even for a moment. That moment came not through peace but through court orders and supervised visits in Beaumont. Still, when I saw their faces light up in unison, it felt like a resurrection. We laughed. We played. We tried to forget time. But after three visits, the silence returned. They stopped showing up. Excuses were made. The joy I tasted slipped through my fingers like sand. And just as suddenly, I learned my son had been moved to Virginia. The court transferred visitation rights, but all costs now fell on me. I tried to reach him— bought him a cell phone, mailed letters, sent gifts. All were dismissed, lost, or returned. His father said the only way to talk was through him. So I stopped hearing from my child. The line went quiet. Last I heard, they were in Colorado. Later, I found out something even more startling—his cousin had married into my own family. The same cousin who had met him at my baby shower. Life, it seemed, had been weaving our stories together in ways I never saw coming.

Then Aaron came back.

He was a name from the past, someone who had lingered on the edge of my life like a bookmark in a chapter I never finished. Over the years, he stayed in touch through Facebook, quietly liking my pictures, sending occasional check-ins. I texted him on the plane ride back to Houston, unsure of what I wanted, only knowing that I needed something familiar.

He met me at an IHOP, and when he hugged me, something in my chest softened. He felt safe. Seen. I introduced him to the kids, and for a moment, I believed that maybe—just maybe—I could start over. But old wounds can whisper louder than new hope. My mother caught wind of our reunion and began planting seeds of doubt, suggesting that no man could be trusted around children. Fear began to crawl back in. Paranoia took hold. I asked Aaron to leave.

We didn't speak for a year after that.

I discovered later that he was married. Another truth that stung—but by then, I was already back in survival mode. David had somehow convinced me to visit for Christmas. It ended the way so many of our chapters did—in chaos. We argued, and I rushed to the airport with the kids, fleeing the tension like it might cling to our skin.

Still, I tried to reclaim normalcy. I enrolled the kids in school and daycare. I looked in the mirror and asked myself: Who do you want to be now?

First, I became a landlord. I rented out the first home I'd ever owned, hiring a management company to handle the day-to-day. Then I studied, passed my exams, and became a licensed insurance agent. When that didn't feel right, I pivoted again—this time, returning to school to pursue my Master's in Business. I poured everything I had into a plan for my own investment company. Every move was a brick in the foundation I was laying for my children's future.

But I still needed space—real space. A home that felt like mine. My mother's presence, even well-meaning, was suffocating. So I reached out to a high school classmate who had become a realtor. We searched Houston, neighborhood by neighborhood, for a house that would reflect the woman I had become.

A few months later, I bought my second home.

Not just a house—but a declaration. A reclaiming. A place where healing didn't have to compete with history.

It wasn't the end. It wasn't even the peace I was seeking. But it was a start.

And for the first time in a long time, that was enough.

Shortly after I moved into the new house, I felt something tug at my heart—a quiet whisper reminding me of Aaron. He had always lingered in the background of my life, never fully gone, always quietly supportive. So I called him. I apologized for the paranoia that had driven him away and explained the chaos I had been navigating. He listened with the same quiet patience that had once made me feel safe, and just like that, we became close again.

Over the next two months, our bond deepened. I dragged him through Disney, Great Wolf Lodge, cruises, outdoor waterparks, theme parks, and any kids entertainment I could find. I watched him carry the weight of his unraveling marriage and the ache of wanting a child of his own. I saw the weariness in his eyes and the gentleness in his voice when he spoke to my children. Eventually, I made the decision to ask him to move in with us. It wasn't just about companionship—it was about healing, about creating a new chapter rooted in something tender, something stable.

He had already begun the divorce process, and though it carried its own storm, we stood together. And eventually, I gave in to the hope he held onto so tightly. I got pregnant. This time we planned every aspect together.

At the same time, I began working at Amazon. My first role was a seasonal, work-from-home customer service position, answering calls from drivers after completing training sessions with videos and virtual group classes. I worked there for about four months before going on pregnancy leave.

We celebrated with a baby shower dressed in blue and gold—soft satin streamers, balloons kissing the ceiling, and tables lined with platters of home-cooked Caribbean food. It was held in our neighborhood clubhouse, a place that finally felt like a safe, shared space. Almost all my cousins and aunts came, flooding the room with laughter and music. For the first time in years, my mother and father stood in the same room, smiling—maybe not at each other, but at me. Aaron's parents were both there too, even though they were divorced. There was tension, yes, but also something sacred in the unity. We danced. We laughed. For a fleeting moment, everything that had been broken stood in the same space, not fixed, but acknowledged—and that was enough. That day felt like a blessing wrapped in rhythm and rice and warmth.

When I returned, they had reorganized the teams, and I was let go. It was a new beginning in every sense—a new home, a new partner, and now a new life growing inside of me. For the first time in a long time, things felt like they were aligning. Not perfectly, but purposefully.

But a few months later, Amazon reached out again—this time with a permanent position on the Amazon Fresh team. I worked my way up, and after a year, I was promoted to the Case Team and eventually became a Logistics Supervisor.

I began to feel a deep, unshakable pain in my side—sharp, then dull, like something buried but screaming beneath the surface. After a few urgent care visits and tests, they discovered kidney stones. I had surgery right before Thanksgiving that year, and I still remember limping around the kitchen, determined to make the holiday feel normal for the kids. But six months later, it happened again. Only this time, it was worse. I tested positive for sepsis and was admitted to the hospital. I stayed there for almost a month— hooked to machines, monitored by nurses, and visited by doctors with grave expressions. I couldn't believe how quickly things had unraveled. My body was waving a white flag, and all I could do was surrender and pray for the strength to recover. Amazon held my job, but the experience left more than scars—it left a reminder that healing is never just physical. It's spiritual. It's emotional. And it's slow.

Once I recovered, I enrolled in the Amazon Choice program, which paid for my college tuition. That opportunity gave me more than just financial relief—it gave me a new direction.

Chapter 23: Jobless, Not Hopeless

I've always been the kind of woman who keeps her promises, even when the world doesn't return the favor. I had just finished my paralegal certification. I pushed through late nights, surgeries, migraines, emotional triggers, and mom guilt to get there. I even made the President's List and yet, that piece of paper didn't come with a key to unlock the right doors.

In August, I started an internship with a small Houston-area law office located in a high-rise building downtown. The attorney, who had contacted me through the school program, was also an instructor at the college where I studied. Beyond teaching, he served on the board of a local charter school and was also affiliated with the metro gas and oil boards. It didn't pay much, but it felt like purpose. He spoke like he believed in my potential. He said I had a sharp mind for contracts and a natural instinct for business law. He told me to stick with him and promised that when the timing was right, he would bring me on permanently.

During my time there, I worked on a range of projects including bylaws, mergers and acquisitions, securities, deeds, and international business law research. He would send me assignments weekly, and after I completed them, I would email them back for review. He proofread my drafts carefully before forwarding them to the clients. The feedback was encouraging, and I grew confident in my drafting skills and legal judgment. Every email felt like a vote of confidence, every revision a chance to grow sharper. I was learning, applying what I had studied, and building a foundation. I believed this was the start of something lasting so much that I walked away from my supervisor position. It was steady, stable, and exhausting. I resigned on December 31, because I wanted to start the new year with intention choosing faith instead of fear.

In January, Trump was re-elected. Just like that, the attorney vanished. No explanation. No offer letter. No returned calls. No text to say he had changed his mind. He accepted a new position with an international firm and left me, along with the promises he made, as if we never mattered at all. That betrayal hurt more than I will ever admit. It wasn't just about the job. It was about what it meant to be left in limbo. I was a mother with four children, no income, no insurance, and no certainty. I felt like I had gambled on my future and lost. All because I trusted someone who spoke like a mentor but moved like a ghost. I refused to believe that my story ended in that struggle. I had survived worse. There had to be something out there. Something aligned with my purpose, even if I couldn't see it yet.

So, there I was, the first week of February. Newly unemployed with a certificate, a laptop, and a heart full of questions. Most mornings, I stared at my ceiling, unsure of what to do next. No job, no calls, no fallback plan. Just a phone that stayed quiet and a mind that would not stop. The fan blades spun rapidly overhead, as if they could somehow blow the weight of my world away. I applied to multiple firms and submitted numerous resumes. Each resume was carefully tailored with experience and education, and cover letters were meticulously crafted with a story full of resilience like my life depended on it. Some responded with silence. Others with polite rejection.

The house was still. Too still. My kids were at school, and I was left with the kind of silence I usually begged for but this kind of silence didn't feel like peace. It felt like pressure. I got dressed just to sit at my desk, scrolling through job boards with swollen eyes and stiff shoulders. I began to question everything. Not just my career choices, but my worth. How could I have believed in someone else's dream for me so easily? Why did I bet it all on words that were not backed by action?

Despite doubts, I kept applying every day. I tried different job boards, updated my LinkedIn profile, created a personal webpage, set up a professional email account, and joined paralegal groups across the country. I applied for and was accepted into the State Bar Paralegal Division, and I began studying CLE trainings that focused on entering the legal field and understanding paralegal ethics. Then, surprisingly, a message arrived. One Thursday afternoon, I got the email I had been waiting for. It was short. It was direct. It was the kind of message that makes your heart skip and your stomach flip. They liked my resume and wanted to talk that same day. I remember staring at the screen and rereading the message like it might disappear if I blinked.

My hands trembled as I read it again and again, trying to decide if this was real or just another detour. I responded within minutes. I looked around my living room, searching for someone to celebrate with. All I saw was the sagging couch, the stack of unopened mail, and the half-eaten breakfast left behind by one of my kids. Everything in me whispered, "Maybe this is it."

I did not know then what this job would bring. I did not know how far it would stretch me or how deeply it would wound me.

But I knew this. I still had hope.

Chapter 24: The Interview

Threw phone rang exactly on time. A young woman introduced herself and asked a few polite questions. She sounded friendly, firm, and in a hurry. I told her about my paralegal certificate, my business law experience, and my internship. I shared that I had four children, that I had left a steady job because I believed in my career, and that I was committed to growth. I even mentioned my migraines, just briefly, so they would not be surprised later. She did not flinch.

We hung up after about thirty minutes. I sat in stillness afterward, unsure of what to feel. Then Friday afternoon, my phone rang again. She asked if I could come in for an in-person interview the next day, on Saturday.

I wanted to say yes right away, but reality stepped in. I could not find a babysitter until three o'clock that day. That night, I barely slept. My mind was full of questions I could not answer. Would this be different? Would they respect me? Would I finally be seen? The interview was already set. I had no choice but to say I would come, even if it meant walking in late.

I didn't have time for hair and nails, but I had my story, skill, and a passion that could not be faked. That would be enough.

I changed my outfit three times. Nothing looked professional enough. Nothing felt like it belonged on the woman I was trying to become. Eventually, I settled on something simple: black slacks, a purple top, and the hope that they would see past the outfit and into the fire that got me here.

I arrived at the office around five in the evening. The sky had started to turn, and the building was quiet. The small law office nestled in a commercial strip, had walls adorned with framed degrees and motivational quotes. Professional. Clean. I walked in and found no receptionist, no one at the front desk offering a welcoming smile. The stillness in the air made me pause. I stood there, uncertain, trying to calm the nerves in my stomach and rehearsing what I would say, knowing there would be no second chances. Then I began to walk around slowly, hoping to find someone. Eventually, I turned a corner and ran into the same voice from the phone.

We will call her Kristy. She gave a brief smile and motioned for me to follow her. She led me into a conference room where another woman was seated. We will call her Kathy, the head attorney. They both invited me to sit down, and the interview began without much formality.

Kathy greeted me with a smile. Her handshake was confident, and her tone was straightforward. She inquired about my experience in probate, guardianship, and family law, as well as my availability, transportation, and disabilities. I told her the truth. I was new to some of it, but I learned fast. I detailed my work during my internship, including document drafting, client calls, and legal research. Additionally, I told her about my goals and my commitment to doing meaningful work. I also disclosed that I suffered from migraine headaches. explaining that I had a prescription and could manage them with proper care. I wanted to be transparent. I also told her about an upcoming trip I had already planned to Hawaii. The family vacation was booked as part of closing my chapter at my last job. It was a personal celebration and a well-earned pause before stepping fully into this new path. She seemed understanding about both. She asked what I was looking for in terms of pay. I hesitated and said it clearly. I would like at least twenty dollars an hour. She nodded quickly and told me my billable rate would be ninety dollars per hour and that I would receive healthcare benefits in 60 days. I was surprised. I understood what billable hours meant, but not yet how wide the gap was between what I earned and what they charged. Still, the number gave me a rush of pride.

Then she said it. "We would like you to start next week, if you are available."

Available? I was beyond ready. I had been waiting for this moment for what felt like forever.

I left that office with cautious optimism. But what I did not know then was that interviews are often not about who you truly are. Sometimes they are about who someone needs you to be. And when people see your light, they do not always want to protect it. Sometimes they only want to use it until it burns out.

This was my beginning. I just did not know how close I already was to the end.

Chapter 25: Day One

I woke up before my alarm. The sun had not even touched the blinds yet, but my mind was already racing. It was Wednesday, three days before my birthday, and my first day in-office as a paralegal. This was the first time I would walk into a law firm, sit at a real desk, and be counted as staff. Not just a helper. Not just a hopeful. Official.

I wanted everything to go right. I had laid out my outfit the night before. Nothing flashy, just professional and neat. I packed a simple lunch, took care of my kids' schedules, and left the house with a mix of nerves and ambition humming through my chest. This was supposed to be the start of something real. A fresh chapter. A chance to step fully into the career I had worked so hard to earn. To show that I was more than just a mother, more than just a woman who had once been stuck in jobs that did not feed her purpose.

I arrived at the office early. The parking lot was nearly empty. The building stood still, tucked into its usual quiet corner. I walked in with steady hands but a racing heart. As soon as I stepped through the entry, I heard voices in the distance of laughter and conversation echoing softly from the back hallway and followed the sounds. I recognized the voices of Kristy and Kathy immediately. They were joined by a few others including a man we will call Tyler, and two women we will call Rebecca and Maria. Their energy was light but enclosed, like a group that already knew how to move around each other.

As I came closer, Kathy noticed me and greeted me from the far back corner of the building. Her office was tucked away, private and polished. She smiled and stood to shake my hand. Her grip once again firm, her tone direct. "Let me show you around." She led me out of her office into the center hub where the three paralegals, Tyler, Rebecca, and Maria had their desks. Each space was small and functional, arranged in a U-shape with a printer at one end and paper files stacked across shared surfaces. The room was quiet, except for the low hum of chatter, a continuous flow of printing, and clicking keyboards. No one looked up right away. Kathy gave a quick wave toward each of them with a quick introduction. Then she pointed to the office next door to hers which was the associate attorney Kristy. "She's right next to me. You'll also work with her closely."

There was an empty office next too hers, two additional conference rooms, two restrooms and a kitchenette. Finally, she led me down the hall, around a corner, and into a smaller office near the front right side of the building. "This is yours," she said. It was quiet, away from the others. The desk was clean but bare, the chair stiff, the computer slow to boot. There was a window, though, and for a brief moment I stared out and told myself this was progress. I sat down, took a deep breath, and prepared to figure it all out on my own.

No welcome packet or checklist. No one hovering to train me or show me the ropes. Just a login list scribbled on a piece of paper and a computer that took its time waking up. I scanned the folders on the desk, trying to get a sense of where things stood. The labels were vague. The formatting inconsistent. Some were missing entirely. There were still a few notepads and documents left behind from whom I assumed was the position I just filled. Various names and statutes I figured I better start recognizing. I told myself to just start. So I did.

A few minutes later, Kristy handed me a password list written on a sticky note. "You'll need access to Clio. Most of the files are digital. Kathy will let you know which ones to pull hard copies for. You'll have access to your own email address, Westlaw, and a RingCentral phone line since you're in charge of the phones for now. Please call our tech support team to help you set everything up correctly and meet us in one hour for the team meeting."

I nodded, trying to absorb everything at once. New faces. New systems. New expectations. I had never worked in this kind of environment before, not officially at least. But I was determined to prove myself. I opened Clio and began exploring and reviewing the client files, templates, emails, and the call center right before the phone began ringing.

My first call was from a woman who introduced herself as a home care nurse. She sounded tense. She explained that she was assigned to assist an elderly woman and had been waiting outside the client's home for nearly twenty minutes, but no one was answering the door. I quickly jotted down a few notes, placed the call on hold, and walked around to Kathy's office. Before I could finish explaining the situation, she waved me off and told me to ask Rebecca instead.

Rebecca seemed annoyed when I approached her desk, but she sighed and explained that the client was one of Kathy's guardianship cases. The court had assigned a nurse to check on her regularly, but the woman's nephew, who had just been released from prison, was refusing to open the door or let anyone inside. She instructed me to email the nurse's agency, inform them of the situation, and advise the nurse to leave the premises for her own safety. I did exactly as I was told. I would come to learn that this exact scenario would become a near daily occurrence. For the next two months, it would be the first call I received most mornings.

The tech support team was hard to reach. When I finally got someone on the line, they walked me through setting up my email and RingCentral account. I wrote down every login, bookmarked every link, and saved backup notes in a folder on my desktop. My screen was already cluttered with windows, reminders, and sticky notes from every direction. Time moved quickly. When it was time for the team meeting, I made my way to the back of the office.

Everyone was already seated in the conference room. Kathy sat at the head of the table, arms crossed, expression unreadable. Kristy was beside her, typing quietly into her laptop. Tyler leaned back in his chair with his arms folded and his laptop open. Rebecca and Maria sat across from them with their eyes down, one on her phone, the other scribbling into a legal pad. No one made space for introductions. The meeting started fast with Kathy rattling off deadlines, client complaints, and hearing dates like she was reading a grocery list. Tasks were assigned without context. She paused only to ask, "Do you understand?" before moving on. I nodded when it was my turn, even though half of it was still unclear. Then Kathy turned toward me and said, "Right now, we are only focused on probate and guardianship, but I have a new business attorney starting soon. That will be your lane once she's onboarded." She then handed me a few printed articles about the probate and guardianship process and told me to begin studying them. No further instruction.

After the meeting, everyone scattered. I returned to my desk and tried to organize my next steps. The calls continued nonstop. Clients asking about court dates, documents, updates, and invoices. Some were frustrated. Some were confused. Many had been waiting for responses no one had provided. I did my best to stay calm, to sound professional, to take detailed notes and flag urgent messages. No one had walked me through the cases, yet I was now expected to manage the communication for all of them. I listened carefully. I documented everything. I tried to match names with files that were either mislabeled or completely missing from the system. I wanted to ask questions, but the energy in the office made it difficult. Everyone was busy or at least seemed like they were.

By the end of the day, I had logged over thirty calls, responded to dozens of emails, updated at least a dozen client files, and completed my first full intake for a new probate matter. My back was stiff. My neck ached. But I felt accomplished.

Still, no one offered feedback or asked if I needed anything. I packed up slowly. The building was quiet again. That same eerie stillness from the morning returned. I stood in the silence, took a breath, and reminded myself that all beginnings are awkward. This was a new world, and I had entered it alone. I told myself it would get better. That tomorrow, someone would acknowledge me. That eventually, I would belong. But now I know sometimes the silence on day one is not awkward. Sometimes, it is intentional.

This is how you learn the line between being new and being seen as disposable.

Chapter 26: Proving Myself

That weekend, my birthday fell on a Sunday. I did not expect anything from work, not even a passing comment, so when I opened the door to my office that Monday morning, I froze. The room was covered in balloons, loosely scattered across the floor in a cheerful mess. A paper happy birthday sign was taped above my desk. A bouquet of fresh flowers sat beside my monitor. The scent was light, almost admirable. It definitely caught me off guard. No one had mentioned anything about it on Friday, but somehow, someone cared enough to do this. This was a small moment of kindness in a space that already felt emotionally distant and I held onto it.

Rebecca was there, as usual, already at her desk with her earbuds in. She had become the one person I saw consistently. Maria appeared approximately every other day and Tyler, who had been present my first few days, was now nowhere to be found. When I asked about him, Rebecca shrugged. "He's always out. Sick with something."

The phone became my first teacher. Every morning, before I had time to catch my breath or organize my thoughts, it rang. Each call introduced a unique issue, an urgent matter, or individual requiring assistance. Topics such as new clients, probate updates, guardianship inquiries, status verifications, and court-related clarifications were all addressed through a single line that no one else seemed to want to pick up.

One morning, a woman's voice cracked through the receiver. She spoke nervously, quickly explaining that her husband had physically assaulted her the night before, but she had no place else to go. She was still in the home with him. Their young son with disabilities had witnessed everything. She whispered between pauses, afraid of being overheard. Her voice shook as she requested someone to help file for divorce.

I stayed on the line. I listened closely, gently confirming her safety. I was not an attorney but, in that moment, I was the only voice on the other side who made her feel less alone. I told her I would make sure she had an appointment, and that I would need to collect payment information to confirm it immediately. I created a client file in Clio, documented the situation with care, scheduled a meeting with Kathy, and added it to the shared calendar. I flagged it with notes to prioritize. She needed protection. She needed direction.

In between calls like hers I kept studying. My background had been in business law and I had taken classes in family and business law during my paralegal studies. My internship was focused on international and corporate matters. Now, I found myself in a completely different field. Instead of discussing contracts or business structures, I was navigating emotional conversations with people caught in the middle of custody battles, grieving over lost loved ones, or struggling with complicated family dynamics. It was a sharp pivot, one I hadn't prepared for but had no choice but to adjust to.

As a member of the State Bar's paralegal division, I had access to CLE trainings on nearly every topic. I took full advantage of that. I returned to the stack of printed articles Kathy had handed me on day one and started playing CLE videos on probate and guardianship law in the background. I paused to take notes, rewound when something didn't make sense, and bookmarked sections I knew I would need to revisit later. It was self-guided, but it was something and I was determined to learn.

Kathy would require me to collect most payments as part of the intake process. If the customer preferred a phone consult, I was instructed to collect the payment information within 24 hours to confirm and hold it until after the call was completed. The attorney would then advise me on the amount of time spent on the call and I processed the payment online. No free consults. If they came in person she would come get me at the end of the meeting and advise me of the amount, then I would then go the conference room and ask the client for their payment information and return with a receipt before leading them out of the office.

Sometimes when I returned to collect payment, I noticed a shift in the clients' expressions. Some looked unsure, others hesitated before reaching for their wallets. A few glanced around, as if silently questioning why someone other than the attorney was asking for their payment. On occasion, I was asked if I worked the front desk or handled billing. I tried not to take it personally reminding myself that I was simply following the office procedure. Despite the awkwardness of those moments, I maintained courtesy and composure. I provided a warm tone and a steady demeanor. I issued receipts, expressed gratitude for their time, and escorted them to the door with professionalism, regardless of any internal discomfort I may have felt.

Kathy wasn't in the office the rest of the week. Rebecca and Maria stayed glued to their screens, earbuds in. Kristy moved quickly between her desk and the copier, barely making eye contact. Tyler, the senior paralegal, said very little. Everyone seemed tucked away in their own worlds efficiently working, but unreachable. I tried not to interrupt but eventually, the silence became too thick to ignore. I needed help understanding how to route calls, where to find appointment slots, and what information I was allowed to share so I again approached Rebecca. She looked up with mild surprise, then sighed. I asked if she could walk me through how the firm handled intake, calendaring, and message tracking and to my relief, she agreed. She showed me how to locate client records, check for conflicts, and assign appointments based on the type of case. It wasn't formal training, but it was something and I clung to it. While others kept moving in their lanes, I was quietly building the map for mine.

Somewhere between the phone calls and quiet studying, I learned that my position came with another unspoken role, the gatekeeper. Because mine was the only office near the front entrance, I was told to always keep my door open. The small window facing the lobby? That stayed open too. It was now my responsibility to greet anyone who walked in before they accidentally wandered past the hallway and glimpsed any confidential files or overheard a sensitive conversation. "Privacy is crucial," Kathy had said. So, I became the unofficial receptionist without the title, without the training, and without ever stepping out of my paralegal role. When the front door chimed, I stood, every time.

Most times it would be an appointment I scheduled myself, or I could see it scheduled on the calendar by another associate. I quickly realized on Wednesdays random elderly people would walk in and stand at the front of the office. When I asked for their name and reason for being here, they either looked at me with bewilderment or confusion because they probably couldn't hear me speak without raising my tone. Rebecca explained that there was another attorney who rented a conference room on Wednesdays and only worked with estate planning clients. I would lead them to one of the rooms ensure their comfort and enjoy the brief moments of small talk that comes with age and wisdom.

One morning, just as I was finishing a call and preparing to log an intake, the front door opened. Kathy had an in-person client meeting. Three men walked into the building, each dressed in rugged jeans, cowboy boots, and stiff button-downs. They looked like they had stepped right off a ranch. Two of them seemed visibly upset with tight expressions, quick movements, and clenched jaws. The third, noticeably younger, wore an ankle monitor over his boot and stood slightly apart, arms crossed. I stepped out from behind my desk and met them before they could look confused or lost, while introducing myself and asking their names. All three looked at me, but not in a warm way. Their eyes scanned me like I didn't belong. Like they were surprised to see a black woman in control at the front of this law firm. I felt it immediately. First the discomfort, then the tension in my chest but I straightened my shoulders, walked forward, smiled professionally, and asked their names again. Then I led them to the conference room without hesitation. They followed, voices low but charged. Kathy didn't need to say much. The rhythm was already understood.

Moments later, I heard them begin to raise their voices behind the glass doors of the conference room. Heated tones, overlapping words, fragments about land, money, and bloodlines. Kathy emerged swiftly from the back and stepped into my doorway. "I need you to sit in and take notes," she said. "This is a probate matter. It'll be a good example for you to see." I nodded, grabbed my notebook, and followed her back in. Inside, the tension was thick. The two older men were brothers. Their father had recently passed, leaving behind a 65-acre homestead. The land had not been divided, but they each lived on separate corners as neighbors. What started as boundary disputes had turned violent. One of their sons had fired a pistol across the property line, hitting his uncle in the leg. He was now seated opposite me at the table, gazing intently as though peering through a mirror. The brothers were here, not just to grieve or divide an estate, but to settle hostility disguised as a legal consultation. I wrote quietly as Kathy took control of the meeting. She kept her tone calm and neutral, guiding them through the basics of probate law, how property was typically handled, and what would be required to bring the matter before a judge. The brothers talked over each other. Accusations spilled. Old resentments came to the surface. I kept my eyes down and kept writing.

After thirty minutes, Kathy abruptly ended the conversation. She stepped out and handed me a stack of paperwork. "Please collect payment and issue a receipt so they can leave," she said. "Then scan the documents, create a client file in Clio as a probate matter, and bill this under 'new client setup,'" before scurrying back to her office and shutting the door. I nodded again and returned to do exactly that. Just me, a folder, and the assumption that I would get it done without delay or error. I processed the payment, issued the receipt, and walked the clients to the door with a calm voice and a steady smile. The moment they were gone, I turned back toward the scanner. I entered their contact information, uploaded every document, built their digital file, and logged the time under the category Kathy had mentioned.

There were no breaks between tasks. As I scanned, the phone rang. As I uploaded, new emails popped in. As I labeled documents, another intake form slid across my desk. Every duty seemed layered with two or three others. Still, no one questioned how I was managing it. The pressure wasn't loud. It didn't come with yelling or criticism. It came in silence. In the assumption that I should already know. In the unspoken message that asking too many questions would make me look unfit. In the way everyone else moved like clockwork and I was expected to keep up or fall behind without complaint. When you're trying to prove yourself, you learn quickly which parts of you must stay quiet so your work can speak louder.

The rhythm of the office started to shift again the following week. A new attorney had been hired. Her name was Mrs. Yoon. She was a young Korean woman with a confident energy, a sharp tone, and a noticeable accent. She had a background in international business law and family affairs. I found her friendly and fascinating. The kind of person who said only what was necessary but carried weight when she spoke. She greeted me politely and thanked me for helping her settle in. I hadn't done much yet, but I appreciated the acknowledgment. Not long after, Kathy called another meeting. This time, once again, it was short and direct. "You'll be working with Mrs. Yoon moving forward," she said, her voice flat but clear. "She'll be handling both business matters and family law." I nodded, hopeful but Kathy didn't stop there. "Until she gets settled, I need you to keep setting appointments for all three attorneys myself, Kristy, and Mrs. Yoon. Also, you're going to take over managing the probate cases A through G."

There was no previous discussion. No opportunity to ask what that meant logistically or whether I'd be provided training or additional support. It was spoken like fact, as if it were already done. I sat there quietly, pen in hand, trying not to look overwhelmed. I wrote it down like I always did, as if it were just another item on the to-do list. But inside, I felt it.

The shift.

My role was expanding faster than I could process. The expectations were stacking without limit. And there was no pause, no check-in, no "Are you ready for this?"

There was just more.

By the end of that first month, I was managing probate cases, the phones, client scheduling, intake, payment collection, document scanning, file creation, and inbox monitoring for three separate attorneys.

And I picked it up without question.

Chapter 27: The Unraveling

March arrived like a storm with no warning. One morning, the calls started coming in harder and faster than before. This time, they weren't probate clients or guardianship caregivers. They were from patients. Patients who were calling from mental health facilities, sometimes yelling, sometimes whispering, often rambling with a desperation that pierced through the phone line. Rebecca explained to me that we had been assigned to the mental health docket for the next month. That meant every involuntary commitment hearing, every emergency intervention, and every call from someone in a fragile state of mind came directly to our office line and directly to me.

The first call that morning was from a man who identified himself as Jacob. His voice was shaky and agitated, flipping between whispers and shouting within seconds. He claimed he was being held against his will after a fight with his brother. "He hit me in the head with a dumbbell!" he shouted. "They all think I'm crazy. But I'm not. I'm not taking their pills. They want to silence me." He then kept repeating that his family was lying to keep him locked away. That the bruises were real but his truth was being ignored. I tried to keep him calm, asked if he would allow me to speak with a family member or someone at the facility. He paused, breathed hard into the receiver, and muttered, "Only if you promise to tell them I'm sane." I promised to do my best. I documented every word and flagged it for Kathy, who still wasn't in the office.

Within the hour, another call came in. A mother, panic in her voice, asking for help locating her son. "His name is Elijah," she said. "He's seventeen. Bipolar. He was violent yesterday and threatened to kill me the moment he gets out. I don't feel safe, but I can't stop worrying. I don't even know where they took him." She gave me his birthdate and begged me to find out which facility he was in. Her voice cracked under the pressure. I told her I would try. I asked if she was willing to let me note her concerns in the file and if Elijah would give permission to speak to her once contacted. She said yes, then broke down into sobs.

Each call layered on the one before it.

Later that week, a woman named Naomi called in from a facility in Houston. Her speech was frantic and slurred with emotion. She had been admitted after a suicide attempt. "I took the pills. I didn't mean to, but I did. Now they have me here. They won't let me see my kids," she cried. "Can you call my husband? Tell him I need to talk to my daughter.

Please." Her fear and grief was palpable. I asked for her husband's contact information and made a note to try to reach him. All I could tell her in that moment was, "You are not alone. Someone will follow up soon."

The final call that week felt like a script from a chaotic drama.

"This is Darren," the man said on the line, exhausted and frustrated. "My wife was just admitted to a mental health facility after she was caught outside our neighbor's house screaming about sex and demanding he 'repay what he owed.' She tried to strip on his porch. The police had to take her in. She's calling me now saying she's going to bring her abusive ex into the picture and tell him lies to take my kids." I stayed calm, listened and took notes. I asked if his wife had given him permission to speak on her behalf and explained our limitations. He sighed. "She said you're her lawyer. I don't know what else to do."

Again, Kathy was not in the office.

Each time I received a call like this, I followed the same pattern, document everything, ask for verbal permission, offer moral support to the best of my ability, and remind the caller that the attorney would be in touch as soon as possible, yet they still called back daily. Nothing about it felt like enough. It didn't matter that I was a paralegal. In those moments, I was the only one picking up the phone, the only one holding space for a crisis. I quickly began to dread the sound of the line ringing. I never knew who or what would be on the other end, only that I had to answer. That someone expected help and I was starting to run out of ways to give it.

Just after Spring Break, I took a long-awaited family trip to Hawaii. I had planned the dates carefully, notified the team well in advance, and made sure all my tasks were in order before leaving. But two days before my flight, Kathy called a sudden team meeting. She was unusually upbeat, pacing the room with excitement as she announced her latest project. She wanted to revamp the firm's website and film a commercial. Everyone was expected to participate, "Friday morning," she said, "I want everyone here. We'll take photos and do a few group shots outside." I reminded her gently that I'd be returning from my trip that same Friday, stepping off an eight-hour flight. But instead of offering flexibility or understanding, she insisted I come straight to the office once I landed. Her tone made it clear that there was no room for discussion. So I did. Still jet-lagged, in vacation-mode clothes stuffed into my carry-on, I drove straight from the airport to the office, smiled for the camera, posed for pictures, and pretended like I hadn't just spent hours in the air with three kids. We had a make-up artist and took a series of awkward photos, while Kathy directed us in between phone calls. We never saw the final product. No follow-up. No commercial. No website updates. It was loudly announced, quietly discarded.

As March pushed on, the calls only grew more unpredictable. It was no longer just clients with legal questions or frustrated family members waiting on updates. Now, it was crying, shouting, pleading, often all in the same call. Some lasted thirty seconds, others dragged on for twenty minutes or more. My desk, already stacked with probate files, new client folders, calendars, and Post-it reminders, became a second kind of triage center. I wasn't just answering phones anymore. I was holding emotional weight I had no professional training for, only instinct and compassion. Nothing could prepare me for what it would feel like to become the first voice people heard in their lowest moments. There were days when I couldn't eat lunch until three. Days when I forgot whether I had logged that last call. Days when the silence after a frantic voicemail felt just as loud as the chaos before it. Still, Kathy remained absent.

The pressure stayed present. And slowly, something in me began to shift.

By April, the weight was no longer just emotional. It was logistical, mental, and physical. I was everywhere. My daily calls now spanned every practice area the firm touched. I was no longer just juggling tasks. I was juggling realities with each one urgent, each one demanding a different version of me. Family law cases were their own breed of chaos.

One morning, I took a call from a woman named Sierra. She was in the middle of a tense divorce with a former soccer player with no legal representation. They had a child with special needs who needed surgery urgently, and she wanted to renegotiate the child support terms before the final hearing. She was direct, yet exhausted, and I could hear the strain in her voice. The pressure of raising a child alone while still fighting for basic support. I listened, documented everything in Clio, and reassured her someone would call her back.

An hour later, a young man named Damien called, eager to set up an estate planning meeting on behalf of his aging mother. He explained that he was planning to move back home to care for her full-time and wanted her to update her will to leave everything to him. He was polite but insistent. "My sister doesn't need anything. She's barely around," he said. I could tell there was tension under the surface. I noted the dynamic carefully and scheduled the consultation.

Then came Angela. She was separating from her husband, and every detail of the division was a battlefield: a beach house in Galveston, a log cabin up north, a five-bedroom homestead, four cars, and a labradoodle they both claimed to love but refused to care for. "I don't trust him," she repeated. "He'll lie to your face and smile." She questioned every invoice, every calendar change, every name on the email thread. Her calls were long. Her tone was sharp. Her emotions ran high.

The next day, I took another call from a man named Glenn, who was mid-divorce and owned a lucrative business. He had several investment accounts but refused to disclose any. "They're in my name," he said. "She doesn't deserve a penny." He called almost daily, inventing new reasons why the documents hadn't been sent yet: a lost password, a closed account, a banker on vacation. I logged every excuse, every time.

But none of them were like Tracy.

Tracy called nearly every week, sometimes multiple times. Each call lasted anywhere from thirty minutes to an hour. She cried. She raged. She whispered. She repeated herself. She described being cut off from her elderly mother by her stepfather and brother, who she said had stolen over $600,000 from her. She said they were hiding her mother, refusing to let her visit and she wanted to petition for guardianship for her mothers' protection.

But then the story would twist.

She said her ex-husband had returned from California to take her kids, claiming she was an alcoholic and abusive resulting in her having to pay child support. That her beach condo had been broken into and ransacked. That no one believed her. That CPS had investigated, and everything was fine, but they kept twisting the truth. She insisted she wasn't drunk or crazy, just angry, hurt, and desperate to be heard. Tracy sent over 100 emails within two weeks. Long ones. Paragraphs stacked on paragraphs. Attachments. Screenshots. Pleas. Threats. Photos of her children. Voicemails she forwarded "just in case." Every time she called, I braced myself. Sometimes I would purposely miss her call, then another paralegal would courteously transfer her back to me. On every occasion, Kathy wasn't in the office, so I did what I had learned to do. I answered with patience, took notes with care. I told her she wasn't alone, someone would be in touch soon, and that I couldn't give legal advice, but I could document every single word she needed me to.

The pressure started catching up to my body by mid-April. My neck ached constantly. My back tensed the moment I sat down, but worse than the physical toll was the mental one. The emotional weight of client stories had begun to root itself in my chest. I couldn't let it go at the end of the day. One day, while juggling back-to-back calls, a sharp migraine began to set in behind my eyes. I tried to push through, but my phone rang again, and this time it wasn't a client. It was a family member calling to tell me my uncle had passed away from cancer. I broke down right there in my office. The pain in my head collided with the heartbreak in my chest, and I couldn't hold it together sobbing uncontrollably at my desk.

Kathy let me leave early that day. I told her that my prescription migraine medication had run out, and I asked if I could activate the health insurance I was promised. She told me I wouldn't be eligible for another 30 days. I was allowed to take three days off, and I spent those days in a dark, quiet room, trying to rest, to process, and to breathe. It wasn't just the headache. It was the grief, the stress, the lack of support all collided at once.

Then came the estate planning assignment. It was the first case I handled from intake to completion unlike the probate matters I had been assigned, which were already in progress when I stepped into the role. I had previous training in legal research and document drafting, and I had grown comfortable using Westlaw in school. Drafting had always been one of my favorite parts of the legal process. There was something deeply satisfying about putting the pieces together, aligning the law with a person's unique situation, and producing something clear and useful.

When they arrived, I greeted them at the front door, guided them to the conference room then went to alert Kathy of their arrival. She looked up from the computer startled and immediately began waving her arms in a 'get out' motion. Confused, I told her the clients were here, and she told me to go wait in the conference room with them because I would be drafting an estate package. Even though no one had told me I would be expected to draft until minutes before the client meeting, I was excited. This one was mine from the very beginning.

It was supposed to be routine. The husband was a tall white man, soft-spoken with a calm presence. His wife, a shorter white woman with warm brown-red hair, carried herself with quiet confidence. Both were retired, a teacher and an entrepreneur with multiple properties and shared that they had only two grown sons. As they spoke, I found myself studying the woman's face. It felt strangely familiar. When her husband mentioned one of their sons' names, it all came rushing back. I had gone to the eighth-grade prom with him. She had also been one of my 8th grade basketball coaches. She didn't seem to recognize me, or maybe she did and simply chose not to mention it. They were kind throughout the meeting. Warm, even. They both made a point to thank me, smiling directly and complimenting my preparation. Their energy stood in sharp contrast to what I was used to. For once, I felt like my work was seen and appreciated.

It felt good until I returned to my desk. I logged into Westlaw and began creating the estate planning package: a will, statutory durable power of attorney, medical power of attorney, and directive to physicians. I carefully tailored the templates to fit the clients' needs, ensuring that every section reflected their wishes. Later that day, Kathy approached me. "Go ahead and bill that estate planning under my name in Clio," she said casually. "We don't want the client confused about who did what." I paused. I had drafted the entire package. Reviewed each section. Finalized the language. I said nothing. I nodded and made the change because at this point, speaking up felt dangerous.

I was doing more than I was hired for. Carrying more than anyone saw and with every task I completed, the expectation quietly expanded. I wasn't being trained. I was being tested and the weight of it was beginning to show. The line between proving myself and losing myself had become dangerously thin. No one officially said it, but I knew I had officially become the catch-all. I was carrying every stray responsibility that didn't quite fit someone else's role.

One morning I came in to find three angry voicemails from different clients each demanding callbacks for things I hadn't been trained to handle. Two emails flagged as "URGENT" were waiting in my inbox before 8:00 a.m. and as usual Kathy was nowhere in sight. When she did appear, it was either for a client meeting I had arranged, a Zoom court hearing, or to sit behind her closed-door rambling on the phone loudly, erratically, sometimes laughing or ranting for hours. Her presence was unpredictable, and her energy tense. She was unapproachable. When I knocked to relay a message from a client or a court clerk, usually something I had already tried to resolve and I only brought to her because it needed an attorney, she would wave me away with an aggressive hand signal or bark, "Not now," without even looking up. If I did manage to get a few words out, sometimes she would cut me off mid-sentence with a snarky comment about how "people call about non-emergencies all day," or how "everyone is so annoying and needs to get a life." Once, when I interrupted her call to deliver an urgent message from a court clerk, she glared at me like I had committed a crime and hissed, "Do not interrupt me when someone else is speaking." There was never a moment of calm exchange. There was no sense of mentorship or calm guidance. Just lots of friction.

Her appearance, too, contradicted my idea of a professional leader. Most days she didn't dress like the managing attorney of a firm. She came in wearing wrinkled tops, jeans, and sometimes her hair barely brushed. It might not have mattered to anyone else, but to me coming in every morning polished and prepared, it felt like a quiet insult. Like the effort I put in was not mirrored by the one who set the tone for us all.

After each encounter, I would nod, say "Okay," and quickly exit her office. But inside, I felt dismissed. Unseen. Like the endless tasks I was juggling didn't count in her world. I would hover outside her door, listening to gauge her tone, weighing whether it was worth the scolding just to pass along a message someone else could ignore. It became a constant calculation of when to speak, how to say it, and whether I could even afford the emotional toll of one more confrontation. The truth was, I had more access to the clients than I ever had to the attorney I worked for and when the person who's supposed to lead you makes you feel like a burden, you stop asking for direction.

Another incident unfolded that further emphasized the intensity of my environment. One afternoon, a large, angry man burst through the front door, demanding to speak to Kathy immediately. He looked like he had just come off a construction site, tall and rugged with a booming voice that echoed through the office. I tried to maintain calm and asked for more information so I could schedule a consultation. He grew louder, insisting that Kathy had probated the wrong will and that what she had done was illegal. He shoved a stack of papers into my hands and told me to read them. Before I could glance at the top page, Kathy appeared from the back, snatched the documents from me, and told the man to leave or she would call the police. He confronted her briefly, still yelling, and then stormed out. I stood there stunned. There had been no protocol, no debrief, just more tension layered onto an already volatile workplace.

Each day at the firm brought a new lesson, sometimes in law, more often in endurance. Through it all, I kept showing up, kept learning, and kept holding on to the hope that all this effort meant something bigger was ahead. My body started to respond to the stress. Tension headaches. Trouble sleeping. I couldn't focus when I got home. I was finally receiving the health care benefits yet it seemed even with medication my body ached. I'd sit down to help my kids with their homework and find myself staring blankly at their papers, still mentally logged into Clio. I stopped talking about work at home altogether and yet the pressure kept climbing. Every call felt like a test. Every client question, a pop quiz I couldn't afford to fail. Every intake had multiple layers of custody battles tangled with trauma, wills clouded with suspicion, siblings accusing each other of theft, children stuck in the middle of it all. Clients cried. Clients yelled. Clients begged while I struggled to stay steady through all of it.

Until Memorial Day.

We had just returned from the firm's first official Monday off, and I arrived Tuesday morning expecting a normal catch-up day. But the moment I sat at my desk, Kathy stormed toward me. Her voice was sharp, eyes locked on mine. "I need to ask you something," she said, loud enough for others to hear. "Did you use our Westlaw account to research family law statutes in Tennessee?" I blinked, confused. "No, I haven't logged into Westlaw at all," I replied honestly. "I haven't been assigned any research tasks." She crossed her arms. "Well, there's a $5,000 charge on the account. Someone accessed a subscription I don't have, and the activity shows it happened recently from your computer." My heart dropped, not from guilt, but from the shock of being accused. Before I could speak further, she cut me off and immediately called a team meeting. Everyone was summoned to the conference room, where she stood at the head of the table and repeated the accusation broadly without naming names. "There's been misuse of our Westlaw account," she said coldly, "Someone accessed a premium database without authorization. I need everyone to change all of your passwords. We've discovered that former paralegals still had access to our systems, and this can't happen again."

The tension was thick. No one looked at me. No one defended me, but I knew the implication had been made. She never brought it up again. No apology or confirmation that I had, in fact, done nothing wrong but the next week, I noticed something strange. Three new cars appeared in the parking lot. Kathy pulled in driving a sleek new luxury Lexus SUV. Rebecca showed up in a shiny crossover with dealer plates still on. Ms. Yoon, too, was suddenly behind the wheel of a brand-new Volvo sedan. I said nothing but, in my gut, I knew.

The pressure wasn't just professional anymore. It was personal. I was in a place where image mattered more than truth, where silence could bury you, and where the people in power would protect themselves no matter who got blamed in the process.

And now, the unraveling had a name.

Distrust.

Chapter 28: The Day It Ended

Thursday started like most days at the firm. Despite a debilitating migraine that affected my vision and focus, I worked until the pain became unbearable. After getting permission from Kathy, I went home early with plans to return first thing in the morning. I didn't want to miss the day entirely because I had already confirmed six client meetings and two document signings. The idea of leaving those unattended, of adding more pressure on someone else or having to reschedule again, felt worse than the migraine itself.

The next morning, I texted Kathy to let her know I would be taking another dose of medication and would head in once I felt well enough to drive. That's the thing about Sumatriptan: it works, but it takes time. It dulls the pain enough to function, but it also slows me down. My head feels heavy, my stomach a little unsettled, and my reactions a bit delayed. Driving required focus and caution, and I waited until I was absolutely sure I could make the thirty-minute commute safely.

I arrived at 9 a.m., just as our first client was pulling up. Her name was Marisol. She was a short, older Hispanic woman with a strong voice and an assertive presence. Kathy had rescheduled her appointment multiple times, describing her as "challenging" and "unpleasant." Nonetheless, it was clear that she required legal counsel for her upcoming divorce hearing by her repeated calls. We entered the building together, and I greeted her before directing her to the conference room. I clocked in after ensuring she was settled. My head still throbbed lightly, and focusing required more effort than usual yet I pushed through it.

After Marisol's meeting with Kathy, the two of them came into my office. Kathy asked me to schedule a follow-up appointment for her to return, and then unexpectedly, they began talking about their outfits. Marisol laughed and mentioned something about her shoes, while Kathy commented on the color of her blouse. It was a strange, out-of-place moment. After everything, they both turned and walked out without saying goodbye. I sat there in silence for a moment, unsure what to make of it. I had barely recovered enough to get through the morning, and yet somehow, the weight of that interaction stuck with me. The way they moved on so casually, as if I was invisible. As if my effort to show up and push through didn't deserve even a simple acknowledgment.

The rest of the day unfolded like so many others before it. I kept moving, even as the slight dizziness and dry mouth effects of my medication and that faint tension behind my eyes that let me know the migraine wasn't fully gone lingered in the background. I answered the phones with my usual calm tone, taking messages and transferring calls. I sent follow-up emails, scheduled appointments, organized documents, and walked clients in and out of the conference room. I checked Clio for updates, logged call notes, and even made sure the office supplies were stocked while I waited for the next client to arrive.

By mid-afternoon, I was holding it all together, unaware that it was already unraveling. I was focused on making sure every appointment was in place, that follow-up calls were returned, that billing entries were made in Clio. I had already helped coordinate two signings, fielded a difficult call from a family member involved in a contested guardianship, and rescheduled an appointment for a client who forgot they had a consult. It was a steady rhythm, the kind of multitasking I had grown used to. Even in the quiet moments, my mind was moving through a checklist. Kathy was in and out of her office, as usual, barely speaking. Kristy passed my desk a few times, silent and neutral. Nothing about their behavior felt different. I had no reason to think anything was brewing behind the scenes.

There had been an interaction that stuck in my mind. Kristy had a new client meeting regarding a TOD (Transfer on Death) deed for a man who was in the hospital. His daughter wanted to ensure the property would transfer smoothly and was trying to figure out how to pay the retainer. When she called back to ask about payment, Kristy happened to be standing in Kathy's office. I asked them both what to tell her. Kathy responded that I should take the payment in cash, which struck me as odd since I had never accepted a cash payment before. I relayed this to the client's daughter, who said she had a joint account with her father and wanted to use that instead. I returned to the office to clarify. Before I could even speak, both Kathy and Kristy looked visibly annoyed. Kristy insisted I take cash, but Kathy ultimately said it would be fine to use the account since the father's name was on it. She waved me off without further explanation. So, when I heard my name and was asked to come to the conference room around 4 p.m., I didn't think twice. I grabbed my notepad and walked in, expecting maybe a scheduling question or a case update. Instead, what was waiting for me would change everything.

Kristy was already seated at the table beside Kathy, who had a notebook in front of her covered in messy scribbles. I sat down across from them. The lights felt too bright, and my migraine began to pulse again. I still wasn't sure why I had been called in.

Kathy got straight to the point. After informing the other paralegals to cover the phone for the first time she probed bluntly, "Do you smoke weed?"

I blinked, confused. "What?"

She repeated the question, then added with a slight smirk, "You know, you guys use it for headaches."

It hit me like a slap. "You guys." I was the only black woman in the office. My locs, my Caribbean background, my presence in that space suddenly felt under a microscope. Her words weren't just a question about medication. They were loaded with stereotype. I could feel the weight of every assumption pressing against me in that moment.

I sat there stunned but answered calmly. I told her I took prescription medication, specifically sumatriptan, for migraines. That was the only thing I had taken. Nothing else. She claimed she had received complaints that I "smelled like weed." I was stunned. I explained that I was extremely mindful of how I presented myself, especially as the first point of contact at the firm. I wore clean clothes, I kept myself groomed, and I always carried scented lotions, body sprays and perfume in my purse. That morning, I was also managing my menstrual cycle and being extra careful about personal hygiene. Once again, none of that seemed to matter. The accusation was already planted. And the undertone was clear.

She leaned back slightly, still holding her notebook filled with what looked like scribbles more than notes, and moved on as if none of it needed clarification.

"You've been off too many days," she said.

I took a deep breath. "I've only taken time off for my migraines, for my graduation, and my son's graduation." I spoke clearly, trying to stay composed. "The only other time I asked off was for July. We sat together and looked at the calendar. You agreed the week of the thirteenth would be best and I put 3 days off on the schedule calendar today."

She paused, then tilted her head and said sharply, "This is a professional office. We can't accept unprofessional behavior."

I didn't even know what she was referring to anymore. What part of any of this was unprofessional? Taking medically necessary time off? Mentioning a family trip well in advance? I felt the heat rise in my body but stayed silent. I just nodded and said, "Okay."

At that moment, I still believed this was a tense conversation, maybe some type of warning, but not a dismissal. I had been working on an estate planning package earlier that day and had every intention of finishing it before I went home. I thought we would wrap this up, clear the air, and keep going.

But then she delivered the final blow.

"Pack your stuff up. Today will be your last day. Do you have any questions?"

I froze. The room went quiet except for the pulse of my migraine thudding behind my eyes. I stood up slowly, trying to understand what was happening. I had shown up every day. I had worked through pain, chaos, and uncertainty. I had taken care of clients. I had kept her office moving and in return, I was discarded with a sentence. Holding back tears, I said, "I can't do that right now."

Krisy, who had been completely silent the entire time except to back up the claim that I had already requested and confirmed the time off on the schedule, suddenly stood up and ran out of the room toward her office. As I gathered my things, Kathy muttered something along the lines of, "She's probably going to hide in her office so you don't feel embarrassed."

The irony. After everything I had endured the migraines, the overwork, the lack of training, the racial undertones, the quiet silencing of my presence, I was supposed to feel embarrassed? No warning or write-up. No conversation about my performance or support. Just an accusation, a promise for an excellent referral, a final sentence, and the door.

I looked at her, my mind spinning from the shock, and I said calmly, "I'm leaving." I grabbed my purse then I walked out. Outside, the world felt quieter than it had in weeks. The buzzing phones, the client trauma, the scattered files, the pressure to prove myself all fell silent.

But inside me, something louder had begun to rise. It wasn't just the end of my job. It was the end of the silence I had been swallowing for months. This was the moment I realized I had never been part of the plan. I had been a placeholder, a buffer for her chaos, a disposable piece in a system that only valued silence and survival.

And now I had a story to tell.

Chapter 30: Rising From the Quiet

The day following my termination, I spent an extended period in quiet contemplation. Not because I was lost, but rather because I had achieved clarity. Leaving the firm should have felt like failure. At least, that's how it was delivered to me. For months I carried a weight that didn't belong to me and the moment I put it down, I felt something unfamiliar but powerful, peace.

The truth is, with barely a conversation, no opportunity for feedback, and a vague, veiled accusation, I was dismissed like I hadn't poured my energy, intellect, and heart into that role. What happened to me wasn't just about a job. It was about the quiet, insidious ways discrimination weaves itself into professionalism. I was a black woman in a white-led office, managing the front lines without support, fielding hundreds of calls, holding space for grieving families, mental health crises, legal chaos all while managing my own health and yet, the moment I showed any sign of needing care or space, I became disposable.

That is the trauma so many of us carry. When you're both highly capable and painfully human, and only one of those is allowed to exist at work. I didn't fall apart. I chose to rise because this chapter is not about how I was treated, it's about how I chose to respond. With reflection. With power. With purpose.

To the new paralegal entering this field learn to listen to the quiet signs early. If you are frequently excluded from support, if your questions are consistently dismissed, or if your presence is regarded as inconvenient, make a record of these occurrences. If leadership becomes defensive when you establish boundaries, or if your well-being is neglected in favor of performance, it is important to take notice. Learn the law but also learn your limits. Take pride in your work but never forget to protect your peace. You belong in this profession but more importantly, you belong to yourself first.

Disrespect doesn't have to come in the form of slurs or screaming. Sometimes it comes dressed in silence, in passive-aggressive comments, in missed opportunities, in false promises of growth that never come. Sometimes it's smiling in your face while slowly stripping you of the dignity you walked in with but you don't have to internalize it. You are allowed to advocate for yourself. You are allowed to ask for training. You are allowed to say no. You are allowed to pause and reassess. You are allowed to leave. If you ever find yourself in a place that makes you question your worth remember, your value is not defined by someone else's failure to see it.

My journey didn't end at that conference room table. It began the moment I walked away from it. Now, I carry a deeper sense of purpose. Not just to succeed, but to protect my peace while doing so because surviving a toxic workplace is one thing. Transforming that experience into wisdom is another. I chose the latter.

And I will keep choosing it every time.

www.ingramcontent.com/pod-product-compliance
Lightning Source LLC
Chambersburg PA
CBHW051136120626
46547CB00012B/828